Reading & Writing With Picture Books

T5-CCV-824

Table of Contents

www.themailbox.com

©2003 by THE EDUCATION CENTER, INC.
All rights reserved.
ISBN# 1-56234-528-1

Manufactured in the United States
10 9 8 7 6 5 4 3 2 1

Reading & Writing With Picture Books

Using Literature to Reinforce Essential Skills

Reading & Writing With Picture Books provides a solid, kid-pleasing foundation for your reading and writing instruction! Literature can open up new worlds for students and can be used to teach a variety of reading and writing skills and strategies. In *Reading & Writing With Picture Books,* you'll find the inspiration and information you need to set up meaningful reading and writing experiences that reinforce essential literacy skills and promote the use of reading comprehension strategies.

Seven Benefits of Using the Activities in This Book

1. When children hear stories read aloud as suggested throughout this book, they are freed from the word-identification tasks involved in independent reading and can **devote more attention to comprehending the stories** using their prior knowledge.
2. Reading or listening to stories, writing in response to them, and getting involved in discussions **enhance children's abilities to understand the things they read.**
3. Reading nurtures writing performance. Writing nurtures reading skills. Relating reading and writing experiences as the activities in this book suggest **prompts growth in both areas,** while also positively influencing students' **thinking skills.**
4. When children hear the same story read aloud several times (as is suggested in this book), they begin to notice things they didn't notice during the first reading. Rereading helps students **understand how the author shaped the story** and gives them **ideas to use in their own writing.**
5. Conversations about stories **provide opportunities to model the use of reading strategies**—such as making connections, visualizing, and inferring—and to **assess which reading strategies children are using and how effectively they are applying them.**
6. When children write in response to reading, they use what they know about reading and writing in ways that are personally important and **meaningful.**
7. The types of goal-oriented and engaging activities included in this book also help children **view reading and writing as purposeful, pleasant experiences and increase their interest in literacy activities.**

Before Reading

- Activate prior knowledge by discussing with students what they know about the picture book's subject matter.
- Set a purpose for reading by encouraging students to predict what will happen or have them listen with a specific purpose in mind.
- Alert students to any new or unfamiliar vocabulary that appears in the text.

During Reading

- Set an example for students and make the text more engaging by reading with emotion and excitement.
- Talk aloud about what you're reading and what you're thinking about as you read. Make predictions and summarize events as you go. Think aloud by verbalizing the questions you have about the text. Also mention what you're inferring and what you're visualizing. Encourage students to use these strategies too.

After Reading

- Lead students in a discussion of the story. Then follow up with one or more of the activities in *Reading & Writing With Picture Books*!

Included in This Book

Reading & Writing With Picture Books includes 12 units. In each unit, a different high-quality literature selection is used as the starting point for a collection of skill-based reading and writing activities. The format of this practical reference allows you to choose featured books and accompanying activities based on your students' needs and interests. Within each unit, you'll find the following elements:

book summary
reading activities
writing activities
skills information

center
reproducibles
icons

Each **book summary** gives you an overview of the book. Three **reading activities** enhance your students' understanding of specific, grade-appropriate reading skills and strategies. Three **writing activities** help students improve their writing skills while reflecting on the story and creating written responses related to it. A featured **skill or strategy** is highlighted above each activity title, making this an at-a-glance resource for preparing lesson plans. In addition, reading and writing skills grids can be found on pages 78 and 79 to use as quick and easy references. One **center** activity that highlights a reading or writing skill is provided in each unit. You'll also find **reproducibles** that can be used to enhance specific activities, to provide individual practice, or to give quick assessments of understanding. Each reading, writing, and center idea is clearly marked with an easy-to-read **icon**.

Reading

Writing

Reading or Writing Center

Reading & Writing With Picture Books

Managing Editors: Kelly Coder, Angie Kutzer
Editor at Large: Diane Badden
Contributing Writers: Kay Baker, Lisa Buchholz, Peggy Campbell-Rush, Rhonda Dominguez, Diane Gilliam, Lucia Kemp Henry, Kim Love, Leigh Anne Rhodes, Lynne Celli Sarasin
Copy Editors: Karen Brewer Grossman, Amy Kirtley-Hill, Karen L. Mayworth, Debbie Shoffner
Cover Artist: Nick Greenwood
Art Coordinator: Clevell Harris
Artists: Pam Crane, Theresa Lewis Goode, Nick Greenwood, Clevell Harris, Ivy L. Koonce, Sheila Krill, Clint Moore, Greg D. Rieves, Rebecca Saunders, Barry Slate, Donna K. Teal
Typesetters: Lynette Dickerson, Mark Rainey

President, The Mailbox Book Company™: Joseph C. Bucci
Director of Book Planning and Development: Chris Poindexter
Book Development Managers: Cayce Guiliano, Elizabeth H. Lindsay, Thad McLaurin, Susan Walker
Curriculum Director: Karen P. Shelton
Traffic Manager: Lisa K. Pitts
Librarian: Dorothy C. McKinney
Editorial and Freelance Management: Karen A. Brudnak
Editorial Training: Irving P. Crump
Editorial Assistants: Hope Rodgers, Jan E. Witcher

Rosie's Walk

Written and illustrated by Pat Hutchins

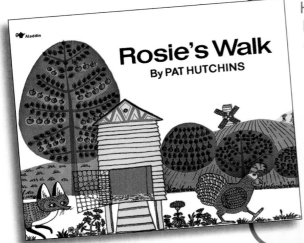

How do you outfox a fox? Rosie the hen does it effortlessly in this amusing story. As she takes a walk through the barnyard, she never suspects that a fox is trying to pounce on her. It just so happens that Rosie stays one step ahead of this not-so-clever fox as he suffers a series of unfortunate mishaps.

Prediction

Let's Predict

Give your students an opportunity to forecast what happens in the story with this warm-up exercise. Show children the book's cover and ask them to describe what they see. Then have a volunteer read the title before asking students what they think the story will be about. Point out the two main characters on the cover and discuss what the students know about foxes and hens and how well they get along.

Share the first two pages of the text with students. Ask how the illustrations could be helpful in predicting what might happen next. Provide time for volunteers to share their predictions with the class. Then turn the page to see if they are correct. Read the next page and stop again to discuss what's happening before students predict what will happen next. Continue in this same manner for the remainder of the book.

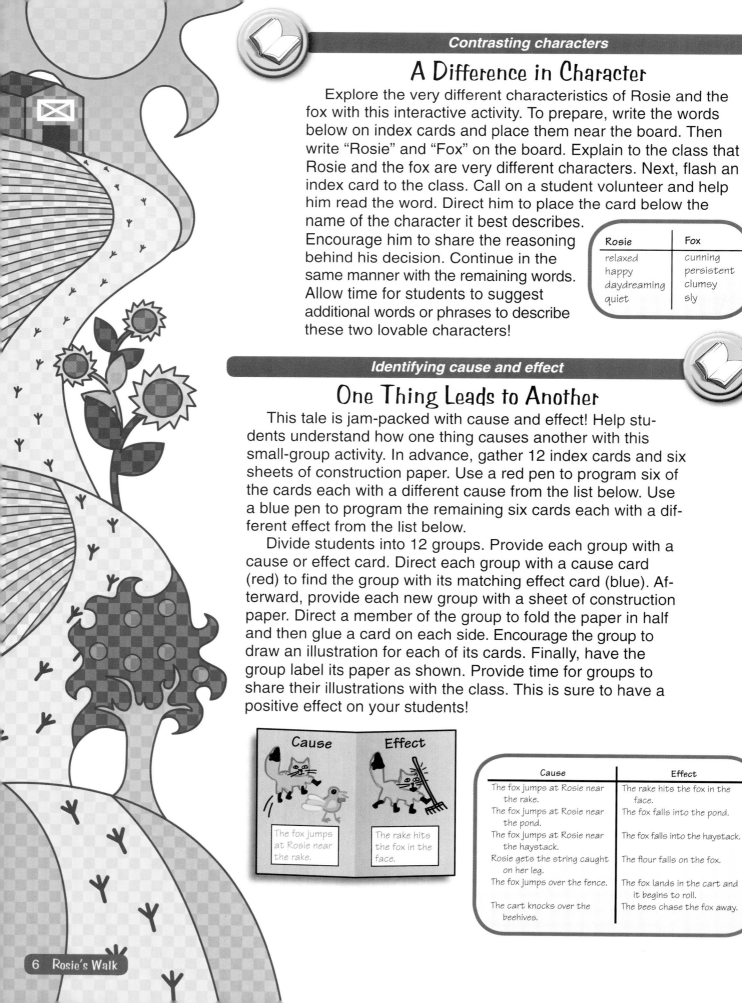

A Difference in Character

Explore the very different characteristics of Rosie and the fox with this interactive activity. To prepare, write the words below on index cards and place them near the board. Then write "Rosie" and "Fox" on the board. Explain to the class that Rosie and the fox are very different characters. Next, flash an index card to the class. Call on a student volunteer and help him read the word. Direct him to place the card below the name of the character it best describes. Encourage him to share the reasoning behind his decision. Continue in the same manner with the remaining words. Allow time for students to suggest additional words or phrases to describe these two lovable characters!

Rosie	Fox
relaxed	cunning
happy	persistent
daydreaming	clumsy
quiet	sly

One Thing Leads to Another

This tale is jam-packed with cause and effect! Help students understand how one thing causes another with this small-group activity. In advance, gather 12 index cards and six sheets of construction paper. Use a red pen to program six of the cards each with a different cause from the list below. Use a blue pen to program the remaining six cards each with a different effect from the list below.

Divide students into 12 groups. Provide each group with a cause or effect card. Direct each group with a cause card (red) to find the group with its matching effect card (blue). Afterward, provide each new group with a sheet of construction paper. Direct a member of the group to fold the paper in half and then glue a card on each side. Encourage the group to draw an illustration for each of its cards. Finally, have the group label its paper as shown. Provide time for groups to share their illustrations with the class. This is sure to have a positive effect on your students!

Cause	Effect
The fox jumps at Rosie near the rake.	The rake hits the fox in the face.
The fox jumps at Rosie near the pond.	The fox falls into the pond.
The fox jumps at Rosie near the haystack.	The fox falls into the haystack.
Rosie gets the string caught on her leg.	The flour falls on the fox.
The fox jumps over the fence.	The fox lands in the cart and it begins to roll.
The cart knocks over the beehives.	The bees chase the fox away.

Adding Adjectives

Enhance the simple, basic text of this story by having your students add a little word power to Rosie's walk! Review the purpose of *adjectives,* or describing words, with your youngsters. After discussing several examples, write "across the yard" on the board. Show the book's illustration of the yard and encourage your students to suggest descriptive words that tell more about it. Record student responses on the board. Repeat the phrase, inserting a different adjective each time. Continue in this manner with the remaining text from the book. Next, have each child choose a phrase to rewrite. Direct him to write the phrase on story paper, inserting his own adjectives to make his phrase more descriptive. Allow time for students to illustrate their new and improved phrases. Afterward, give each student an opportunity to share his work with the class. If desired, use the new phrases and illustrations as you reread the story.

Rosie the hen went for a walk across the large, flat yard.

Josh

Speaking Up

Get students thinking about what the two characters in this story might be thinking with this writing activity. In advance, cut 27 speech bubbles from paper. Read the story aloud. Point out to students that in the story the fox and the hen do not talk. Ask a student volunteer to imagine what the fox might say on the first page if he were to speak. Program a speech bubble with his suggestion and clip it near the fox. Next, ask a different volunteer to study the illustration on the opposite page and suggest something Rosie might say. Program a second speech bubble and attach it near the hen. Continue in this manner with the remaining illustrations. If desired, invite a child to read the fox dialogue and another to read the hen dialogue as you reread the story. Now you're talking!

Mmm, I bet that hen would taste delicious!

A New Setting

Rosie's stroll through the barnyard is indeed entertaining, but just wait until your students use their creativity to write a new tale! In advance, program the bottom of six sheets of construction paper each with a different preposition and article from the list below. To begin, review the prepositions used in each example and invite student volunteers to demonstrate them for the class. Next, brainstorm different settings for the story (such as a zoo, jungle, forest, and ocean) and have the class choose one. Then help students list characters that would most likely be found in that setting. Divide your students into six small groups. Allow each group to select a preprogrammed page and a character from the list. Next, challenge the group to complete its sentence by having its character move across, over, under, through, around, or past something that might be found in the chosen setting. Allow time for the group to illustrate its page. If desired, bind the pages into a booklet titled "In the [setting]."

across the
over the
under the
through the
around the
past the

The monkey swung through the trees.

Rosie's Route

This center is a great way to check students' recall of Rosie's walk from start to finish. Ahead of time, make construction paper copies of the body and tail patterns on pages 9–10, and then cut them out along the bold lines. Program the backs of each matching pair with identical stickers (for self-checking) before laminating them for durability. Store the patterns in an envelope; then place the envelope and a copy of *Rosie's Walk* at the center.

In turn, send each student to the center, and direct her to place the patterns faceup. Have her match each preposition and article (tail) to their corresponding place (body). Encourage students to use the book as a reference. Afterward, have the student flip the pairs to check her answers. Now that's fun from beginning to end!

yard

beehives

pond

haystack

Body and Tail Patterns
Use with "Rosie's Route" on page 8.

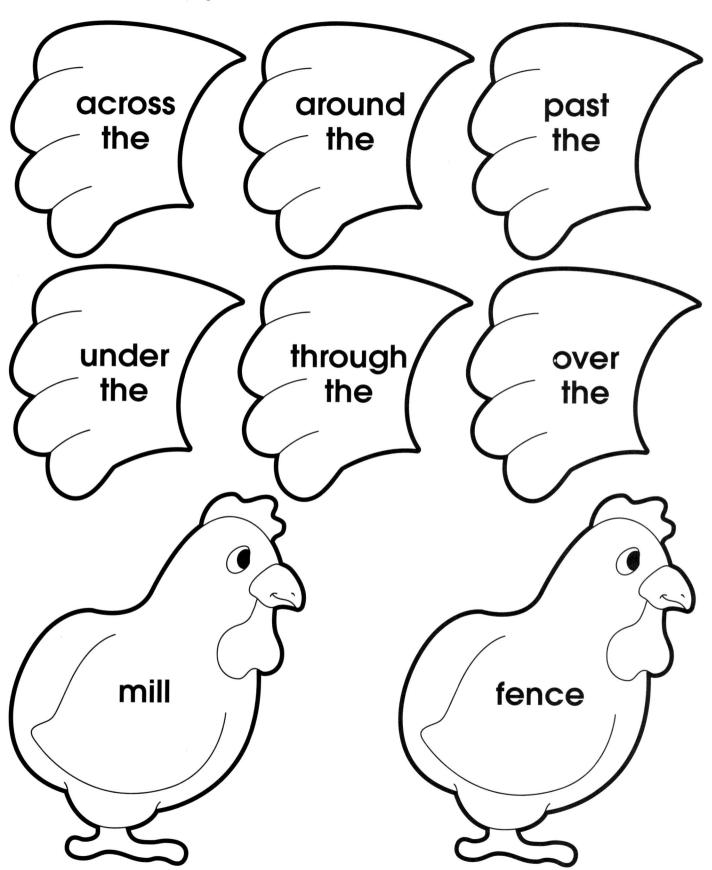

across the

around the

past the

under the

through the

over the

mill

fence

The Carrot Seed

Written by Ruth Krauss
Illustrated by Crockett Johnson

Although everyone around him is doubtful, the little boy in this story believes that his carrot seed will grow. His patience, hard work, and faith pay off when the seed not only grows, but grows into a huge carrot! The reader learns that standing your ground in the face of doubt can often result in BIG rewards!

Word families

Words to Grow On

Carrots aren't the only things growing here! Help students create these adorable booklets and watch word knowledge grow, too! In advance, gather a 12" x 18" sheet of brown construction paper, a 5" x 7" piece of construction paper, a sheet of writing paper, a copy of page 16, scissors, crayons, and glue for each student. Introduce the activity by writing "-eed," "-ay," "-ill," and "-oy" on the board in four separate columns. Review these word families and call on volunteers to contribute several associated words to each column. Continue to add to this list as you reread the story aloud, challenging students to listen for more words *(seed, weed, day, still, boy)*.

Provide children with the materials mentioned above; then provide assistance as they complete page 16 to make word family booklets. On the writing paper, direct each child to use the words to write sentences that tell either something about the story or how she felt about the story.

For a creative display, glue three sides of the smaller piece of construction paper to the brown sheet, leaving the top open to make a pocket. Have the child attach her writing to the brown construction paper and slide her carrot booklet into the pocket. Voilà! This writing is truly a work of art!

My Own Seed Story

This booklet-making activity is sure to get your students' creative juices flowing! In advance, copy the booklet pages on page 15 enlarged to 150 percent on 11" x 17" paper to make a class supply. Tell each child he will be creating an original seed story where *he* is the main character. Guide the student in thinking about what kind of seed he would like to plant and who the other characters in his story would be. Provide each student with a copy of page 15 and allow time for him to write and illustrate his story. Direct each child to carefully cut out each booklet page along the bold lines, and assist him in sequencing the booklet pages behind the cover and stapling it together. Finally, provide time for each student to read his booklet with a partner before he takes it home to read with family members. Write away!

Sorting by Syllables

Invite students to clap, snap, and count their way to a better understanding of syllables with this fun activity! To begin, draw four large carrot shapes on the board, labeled as shown. Remind your students that in *The Carrot Seed,* the little boy successfully grows a carrot. Brainstorm with students other things he could grow. As a student offers an answer, have the group clap, snap, or stomp out the syllables in her word. Then help the student write her word on its corresponding carrot shape. Continue in this manner until everyone has had a turn to respond. That's the "sort" of thing kids love!

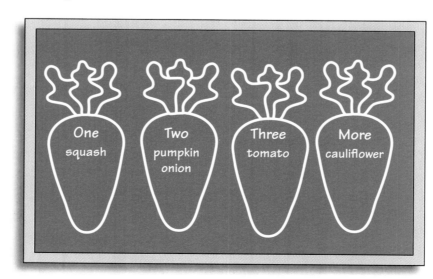

A Class Act

Now appearing in a classroom near you, this dramatic presentation of *The Carrot Seed* tale! After sharing the story with your students, write on the board "It won't come up." Guide students in chorally reading the sentence and talk about its significance in the story. Next, divide your youngsters into groups of four, and assign each group member a different part (little boy, mom, dad, and big brother). As you reread the story, have each student act out his part and read from the board on cue. For example, when you read, "His mother said," students who are playing the mother then read the line from the board. Encourage your youngsters to use imaginary props, such as a watering can, to add to the performance. If desired, have a parent volunteer take snapshots of your students in action.

The Slow Growth of a Plant

Tap into your youngsters' knowledge of plant growth as they complete this scientific writing activity. In advance, gather glue, green construction paper scraps, a 12" x 18" sheet of brown construction paper, scissors, and a half sheet of writing paper for each student. To begin, talk with your students about what they already know about plants and how they grow. Refer to the story and ask students if plants grow like the carrot does in the story. Lead students to conclude that plants do not grow all at once. Then write "nurturing" on the board. Discuss what it means to nurture and how the boy in the story nurtures his carrot seed *(watering and weeding)*.

Provide students with the materials listed above. Direct each child to write (or dictate for you to write) on writing paper a sequential story of plant growth and nurturing. Encourage her to write about how water, sun, and weeding help the plant to slowly grow from a tiny sprout to a bigger and bigger plant with a fruit, flower, or vegetable.

To display her work, help each child fold her construction paper in half and cut the edges to make a pot as shown. Have her glue the sides, leaving the top open, and then glue some crinkled construction paper strips to the top of her writing paper to resemble a growing plant. Finally, she can tuck her writing page inside the pot. Just pull and read!

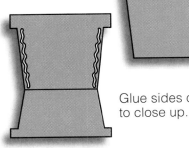

Beans take a long time to grow. First you plant them in

Sarah

Fold.

Cut on dotted lines.

Glue sides on inside and fold to close up.

Words of Encouragement

This little boy's family sure has a lot to say about his carrot seed! Get students thinking about the dialogue in the story with this writing activity. To begin, talk with students about what the little boy's family has to say about his carrot seed. Then revisit the pages of the story that contain dialogue and ask students what they notice about the words. *(They have quotation marks around them.)* Tell students that quotation marks go around what a person says. Brainstorm with students some words of encouragement for the little boy. Call on student volunteers to offer one-sentence encouragements and write each one on the board. (Or, if abilities allow, have the students do the writing.) Afterward, guide the children in converting the sentences into dialogue by adding quotation marks and the contributor's name.

Now read the story again. After reading, "Everyone kept saying it wouldn't come up," insert the encouraging sentences from the children. What a perfectly positive lesson in encouragement *and* quotation marks!

Rachel says, "It will come up. Just give it time."

Billy says, "Keep trying! Don't give up."

From Seeds to Sentences

This tactile center is a great way for students to get a close-up look at seeds while improving their writing skills! In advance, obtain several packets of various types of seeds. Empty each packet of seeds into a resealable plastic snack bag and staple the packet to the bag. Place the bags at a center along with a class supply of 12" x 18" construction paper, glue, crayons, and a supply of hand wipes for quick and easy cleanup.

In turn, each student goes to the center. Instruct him to fold his construction paper into thirds. Next, have him select a bag, remove one seed, and glue it to the left side of the top section of his construction paper. Then direct the student to write beside the seed a sentence describing what the seed looks like. Finally, have the child draw a picture of what the seed will grow into, using the seed packet as a reference. Have the student repeat this process with two other seed bags in the remaining sections of his paper. Remind each student to use a hand wipe to clean up before leaving the center. Encourage students to take their creations home to share with family members.

This seed is very small and brown.

The pumpkin seed is large and oval, like a teardrop.

This seed is black-and-white striped like a zebra.

A Seed

by _____

©The Education Center, Inc.

_____ planted a seed.

1

_____ said,
"It won't come up."

2

_____ said,
"It won't come up."

3

_____ said,
"It won't come up."

4

Every day _____
pulled the weeds.

5

Every day _____
sprinkled water on the ground.

6

And then one day, a
_____ came up.

7

top

Words to Grow On

Glue top of strip here.

by _____

©The Education Center, Inc.

bottom

1. Write your name.
2. Fill in the blanks with words from the board.
3. Color the carrot top and bottom.
4. Cut, glue, and fold.

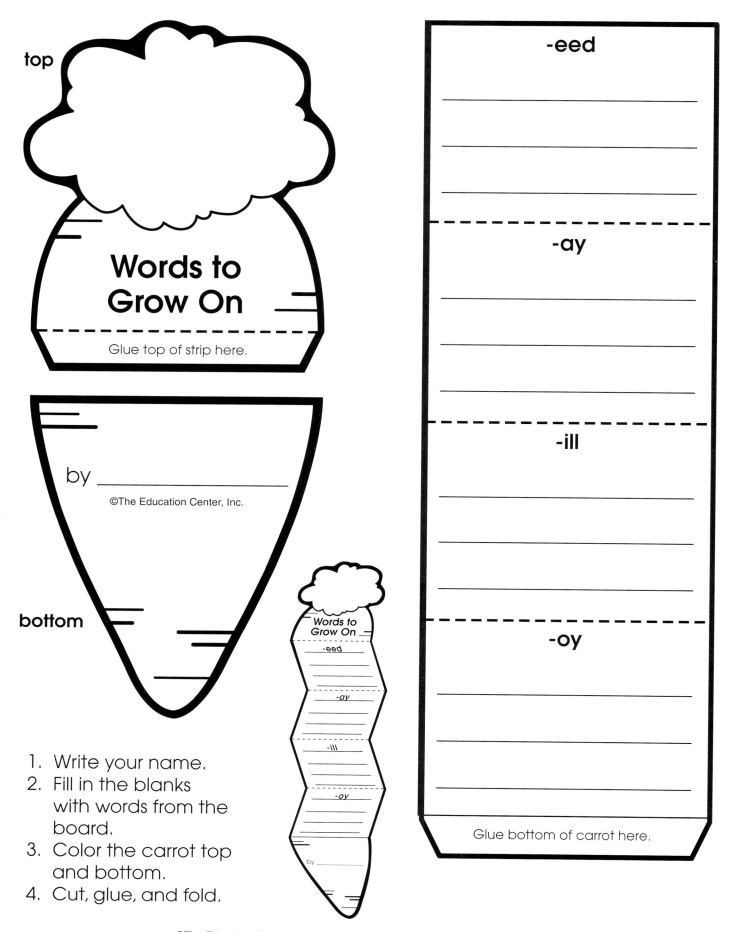

-eed

-ay

-ill

-oy

Glue bottom of carrot here.

Note to the teacher: Use with "Words to Grow On" on page 11. Help students accordion-fold their projects to complete them.

Whistle for Willie

Written and illustrated by Ezra Jack Keats

Introduce your students to Peter, a delightful little boy with a wish. He wishes he could whistle. Peter decides it would be fun to call his dog, Willie, by whistling. All day long Peter blows and blows, but nothing comes out. Finally, through hard work and perseverance, Peter's wish finally comes true!

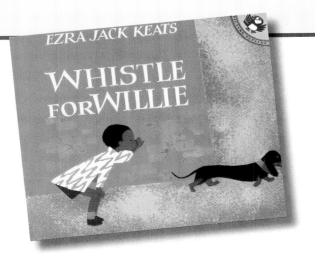

Prediction

Story Forecasts

Get your children thinking ahead as you lead them through this prereading activity. Show the book's cover and ask students to describe what they see. Then have a volunteer read the title before asking students what they think the story will be about. Discuss with your children what it means to whistle, why people whistle, and whether they know anyone who whistles. Next, do a picture walk of the entire book and have children tell what they think is happening in the story just by studying the illustrations. Then read the story aloud. Afterward, review students' predictions to see if they were confirmed.

Then and Now

Give your students an opportunity to tout their accomplishments with this writing activity. Review the story with your students and discuss how Peter feels at the beginning of the story. Talk about how he might feel when he tries and tries to whistle but can't. Contrast those feelings with how he is feeling at the end of the story when he finally accomplishes his goal. Have youngsters brainstorm things that they can do now but could not do when they were younger. Provide time for students to share their ideas with the class.

To complete the activity, give each child glue, two half sheets of writing paper, and a 9" x 12" sheet of construction paper. Next, have him write on one half of his writing paper about a task he couldn't do when he was younger. Then, on the other half, have him write about what it is like now that he is successful with that task. Next, help each child glue his papers on opposite sides of the construction paper. Direct the student to label the "Then" side and the "Now" side of the construction paper. Provide students with self-adhesive foil stars to decorate their creations. Then punch a hole near the top of each paper, tie on a piece of yarn, and hang it for display. Like Peter, they've come a long way, baby!

I Wish I May...

With this unique graphic organizer, your youngsters may find that developing written ideas is as easy as wishing on a star! Remind students that Peter wishes he could whistle, but it takes a while for him to accomplish his goal. Write the word *WISH* on the board in very large letters. Share with students something you wish you could do. Next, erase the *ISH* and label the *W* with question words as shown. Now draw another large *W* and lead students through the process of labeling it with words or phrases to answer the corresponding questions about your wish. Together, turn the ideas into a paragraph by using the words or phrases to write sentences. Then

read the paragraph aloud. Repeat the activity by having each student label another *W* with words or phrases related to his wish and then write his own paragraph. If desired, bind the finished paragraphs into a class booklet titled "More Than Wishful Thinking."

Which Word?

Step into the world of *w-* and *wh-* words with a simple game that students help to create! In advance, program a copy of the parent letter on page 21 and copy it to make a class supply. Have each child complete a copy at home with a parent's assistance. When all of them have been returned, cut each parent letter into two word strips. On the day of the activity, scatter the children's word strips on the floor and invite students to stand around and in between the strips. Then call out a child's name and direct him to step to a strip that is within his stepping distance, read the word, and use the word in a sentence. Then have each student move to a new location. Now ask a different student to step to a nearby word strip and repeat the activity. Continue in this manner until everyone has had a turn. Students will quickly know **wh**ich **w**ord is **wh**ich!

Perseverance Prevails

Take this opportunity to highlight the universal theme of perseverance with this outdoor writing activity. Remind students that in the story, Peter is successful at whistling because he does not give up. He keeps on trying, and he finally accomplishes his goal. Talk to students about perseverance and what it means. Encourage them to give examples of perseverance in their own lives by naming things that were once difficult to accomplish but are now much easier to do, such as riding a bike or tying their shoes. Encourage them to share with the class the frustrations and the joys associated with working hard and reaching goals. Provide each student with a piece of sidewalk chalk and lead him to a section of the school sidewalk or paved area. (If this is not available, provide each student with a large gray sheet of construction paper.) Direct each child to write and illustrate something he can do because he, like Peter, didn't give up. Provide time for each student to read his work and briefly talk about his experience. You did it!

The Things You Do

Boy is Peter busy! Get students thinking about all the things Peter does in this story as you introduce action words. In advance, program each of 16 sentence strips with a different incomplete sentence from the list shown. Also program each of 16 index cards with a different word from the word list. Keep the sentences and word cards separated into four groups as indicated and place them each in a different area of the classroom.

Talk about all the things Peter does in the story. Have students contribute to a list of words from the story that show action. Next, divide students into four groups and send each group to a different station. Direct each group to read each sentence together, think about what happens in the story, and then decide on the correct action word. Upon agreement, have a group member place that word card in the appropriate place in the sentence. Have the group continue in this manner until each sentence is complete. Then direct the group to remove the index cards from the strips to ready the station for the next group. Signal by whistling for the groups to rotate to the next station. Play continues until each group has completed all four stations.

Station 1
Peter _____ under the carton.
Peter _____ on a crack.
Peter _____ but nothing happens.
Peter _____ on his father's old hat.
Station 2
Peter _____ to whistle.
Peter _____ all the way to the store.
Peter _____ into the mirror.
Peter _____ he could whistle.

Station 3
Peter _____ into his house.
Peter _____ his dog.
Peter _____ around and around.
Peter _____ a long, long line.
Station 4
Peter _____ off his shadow.
Peter _____ home.
Peter _____ that he is his father.
Peter _____ chalk from his pocket.

Station 1	Station 3
scrambles	goes
walks	sees
blows	turns
puts	draws

Station 2	Station 4
tries	jumps
whistles	starts
looks	pretends
wishes	takes

From Beginning to End

Try this adorable center that reinforces the proper use of capitalization and punctuation. In advance, gather 12 sentence strips. Next, program each strip with a different sentence about the story. Omit the first letter and the ending punctuation. Now, make four construction paper copies of the dog cards on page 22. Program each card with a capital letter or punctuation mark needed to complete a sentence. Provide an answer key for easy self-checking.

To use the center, have each child complete each sentence by placing the correct capital letter card at the beginning of the sentence strip and the correct punctuation card at the end. When all the sentences are complete, have him use the key to check his work. Now that's fun from beginning to end!

Is Peter here?

Dear Parent,
    We have recently been studying words that begin with *w* as in *wagon* and *wh* as in *wheel.* Please help your child select and write a *w-* and a *wh-* word below and return them to school by _____. Your child will be using his/her words to play a game.

                                        Thank you!

**w-
word**

**wh-
word**

Dear Parent,
    We have recently been studying words that begin with *w* as in *wagon* and *wh* as in *wheel.* Please help your child select and write a *w-* and a *wh-* word below and return them to school by _____. Your child will be using his/her words to play a game.

                                        Thank you!

**w-
word**

**wh-
word**

©The Education Center, Inc. • *Reading & Writing With Picture Books* • TEC1790

Dog Cards

Use with "From Beginning to End" on page 20.

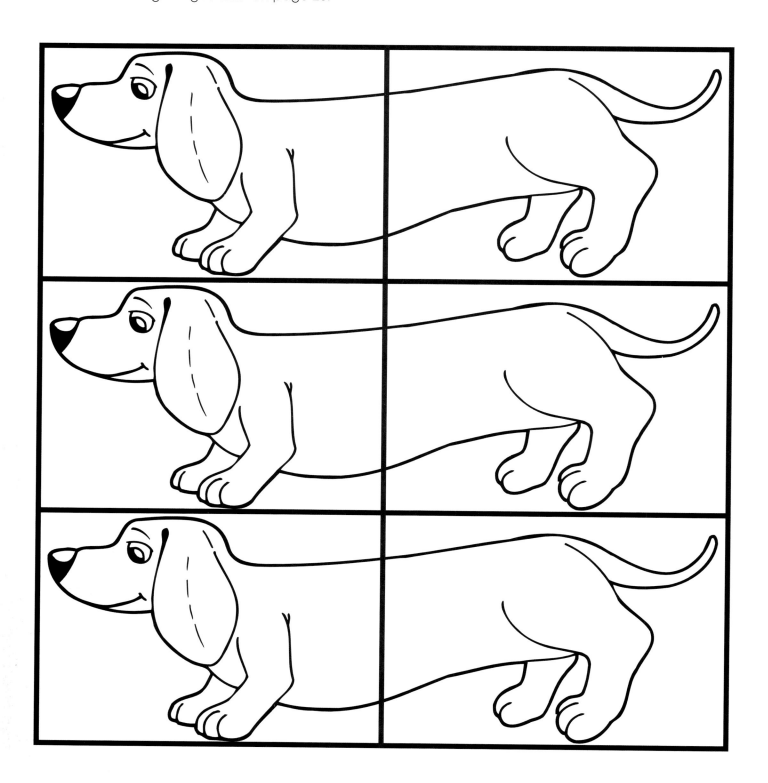

Noisy Nora

Written and illustrated by Rosemary Wells

Nora desperately wants the attention of her parents, but they are too busy with her siblings to notice her. Nora tries everything from making a mess of the house to flying a kite indoors, all without success. Finally, she decides to run away. When her family realizes her absence, they begin searching for her in a panic. But it's not long before Nora comes crashing back, ready to be noticed!

Choral reading

Exclamatory Performance

Try this reader's theater activity and let your students put a little expression into their reading! After sharing the story with your students, point out the text that is repeated (" 'Quiet!' said her father. 'Hush!' said her mum. 'Nora!' said her sister, 'Why are you so dumb?' "). Write it on the board in rebus form as shown. Guide students in chorally reading from the board. Next, point out the exclamation marks and ask the children what they are and what they signify. As you reread the story, signal for students to chime in each time you come to the text written on the board. Encourage the children to read with drama and emphasis, pointing and shaking their fingers as if scolding. Repeat this reader's theater a few times, giving students several opportunities to read, dramatize, and enjoy the words.

Afterward, ask students to be on the lookout for exclamation marks in other readings. Whenever one is spotted, encourage students to bring it to the class's attention and discuss how it changes the reading. Encore! Encore!

Quiet!

Hush!

Nora!

Why are you so dumb?

Yes or No?

Challenge your students' memories with this quick review game. Reread the story aloud. Then help each child create an answer card by folding a half sheet of white construction paper in half to create a stand-up tent. Have the student write "Yes" on one side of the tent and "No" on the other side.

Begin the review by stating an event that did or did not occur in the story. (See the list for suggestions.) If the student thinks the event did happen in the story, direct her to turn her answer card so that "Yes" is facing outward. If she thinks the event did not happen in the story, direct her to turn her answer card so that "No" is facing outward. After each question is answered, ask, "How do you know?" Encourage the children to use the book to support their answers. Continue in this manner with several different events. What a fun review!

Jack needs burping. *(yes)*

Nora drops her sister's candy on the kitchen floor. *(no)*

Mother cooks with Jack. *(no)*

Nora flies her brother's kite down the stairs. *(yes)*

Jack has gotten filthy. *(yes)*

Nora breaks the window. *(no)*

Father reads with Kate. *(yes)*

Nora is in the cellar. *(no)*

They look for Nora in the mailbox. *(yes)*

They find Nora in the trash. *(no)*

Yes

From My Heart to Yours

Help students show their families how much they care with these heart-to-heart mementos. Discuss that even loving family members can say insensitive things and not have time to attend to children's needs, just as Nora experiences. Talk about the love that is evident at the book's end and how important it is to understand and appreciate family members amid the day-to-day hubbub.

For this writing project, have each child choose one family member that he appreciates and would enjoy writing about. Provide each student with a sheet of paper, a 9" x 12" sheet of construction paper, a copy of the heart pattern on page 27, a small heart cutout, scissors, crayons, and glue. Direct each student to color the pattern and cut it out along the bold outer line. Then help him fill in the blank on the heart. Next, have the child glue the lower edges of the back of the heart and attach it to the sheet of construction paper, leaving the top open to create a pocket. Have each student write on his writing paper some of the things he loves and appreciates about his relative. For an added touch, have each student draw a picture of his loved one on the small heart cutout and glue it to his paper. Give each volunteer an opportunity to share his work with classmates before folding it and tucking it into the heart pocket for delivery to the mentioned loved one. These small tokens of love are sure to be appreciated.

I love my brother Sam. We play ball. He helps me bat. I love him. Mike

I love my brother

Dear Nora

With this letter-writing activity, give students the opportunity to help Nora. Tell them that there are several occasions in the story when Nora has to wait. Review each instance and then lead students to conclude that Nora does not behave very well during those times. Give the children an opportunity to share their personal experiences about times when they have had to wait. Together, brainstorm a list of good things to do while waiting. Then have each student write a letter to Nora giving her advice on at least one positive way to wait for her parents' attention. Encourage students to read their letters aloud. Then, if desired, bind the letters together into a class booklet titled "Not-So-Noisy Nora." Place a copy of *Noisy Nora,* the class booklet, and a note summarizing the activity in a large zippered bag and send it home for more sharing.

Dear Nora,
I have an idea! You can watch a video while you wait for your mom.
Love,
Kirke

Dear Nora,
I think if you helped your mom, she would have more time to spend with you.
Love,
Amanda

Rhymes With Family

Two heads are better than one when pairs of students use rhyming words to create these silly sentences. As you reread *Noisy Nora* aloud to students, challenge them to listen for rhyming word pairs. Then list on the board the pairs that share the same word pattern *(door, floor; chairs, stairs; back, Jack; song, wrong, tub, shrub; trash, crash)*. Guide students in observing why these words rhyme; then underline the matching word endings. Pair students and assign each pair two rhyming words from the list. Encourage creativity as you have the pair use its rhyming words to write and illustrate a silly sentence about their own family lives. If time allows, encourage the pair to write more silly sentences with rhyming words.

My family tried to sing the song, but the words came out all wrong!

My sister and I took the chairs and made a tent under the stairs.

Book of Noises

Nora sure is noisy! Get students thinking about what being noisy really means with this booklet-making activity. To prepare, cut a six-foot length of bulletin board paper into three eight-inch-wide strips. Accordion-fold each strip at six-inch intervals and then tape the three sections together to make one continuous strip. Also obtain two 4" x 6" index cards for each child. Ask children what *noisy* means and specifically why Nora is considered noisy. Brainstorm all the noisy actions your students can think of (such as yelling, stomping feet, dropping a tray) and list them on the board. You'll need at least one action per child.

To complete the activity, have each child choose a different noisy word. Provide each child with two cards; then have him write his chosen word or phrase on one card and illustrate it on the other. Glue each child's cards to adjacent pages of the accordion-folded booklet, using the back of the booklet if necessary. This is one class booklet that students will want to read over and over again!

A Word About Mum

Students will use their creative expression as they visit this synonym center. Ahead of time, gather construction paper, several old magazines with pictures, scissors (or pinking shears), glue sticks, and a class supply of page 28. Place the items at a center. Ask your students what they call their mothers, and write their responses on the board. Explain that there are several words that mean "mother." Point out to students that in this story, Nora's mother is referred to by a word that may not be familiar to them: *Mum.*

As each student visits the center, direct him to decide whether to make a mother or father collage. Then have him carefully cut out the corresponding cards along the bold lines. Next, have him cut from the magazines pictures or words that represent a mother (or father). Then have him create a collage by overlapping and gluing the pictures and provided words onto construction paper. If desired, allow each student to create a second collage. Send these works of art home for parents to appreciate.

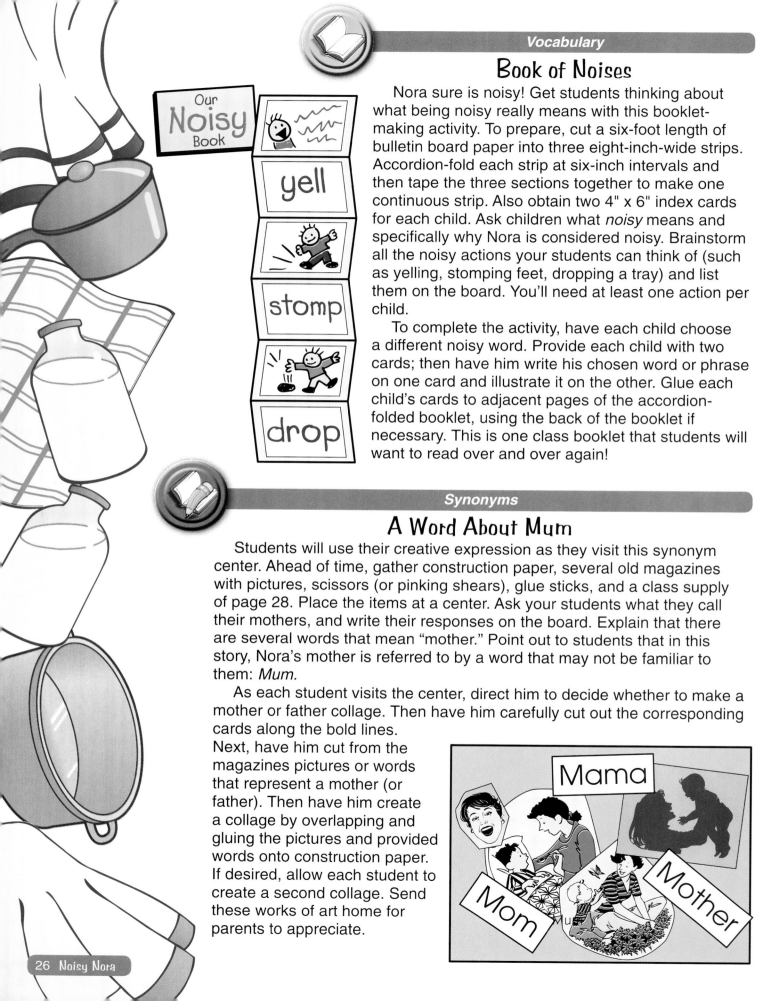

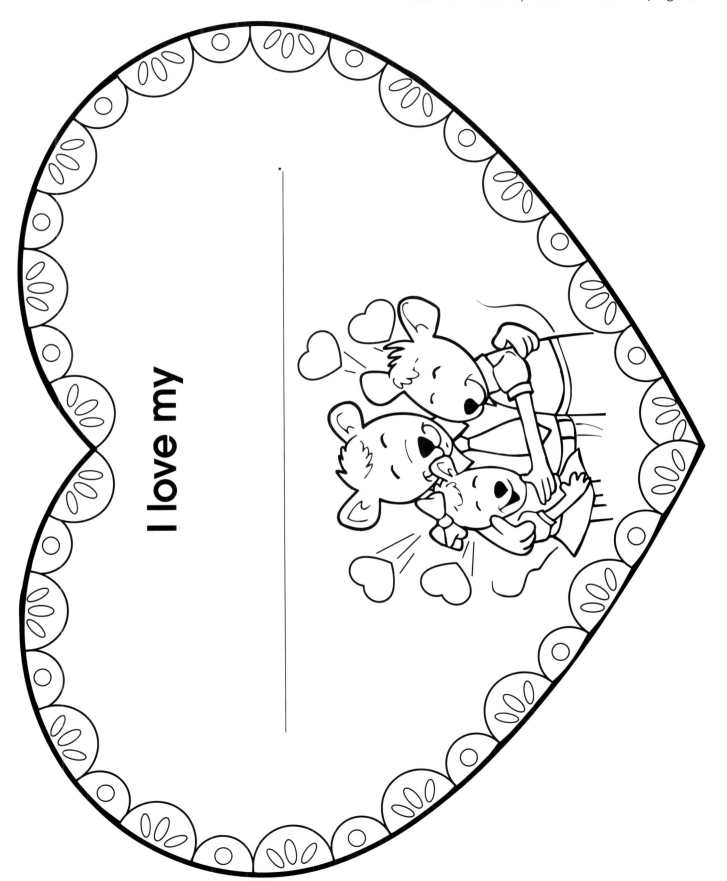

I love my

Mother Cards

Mom

Mother

Mama

Mum

Mommy

Father Cards

Dad

Papa

Daddy

Father

Pa

Note to the teacher: Use with "A Word About Mum" on page 26.

Where the Wild Things Are

Written and illustrated by Maurice Sendak

Max makes all kinds of mischief while dressed in his wolf suit. But he goes too far when he yells at his mother after she calls him a wild thing. She sends him to bed without dinner. Max then uses his imagination to take an exciting journey to where the wild things live. Max and the other wild things have a marvelous time rollicking together, but soon enough, he is lonely and wants to be back where he is loved best. Max returns home to find a hot meal waiting for him. Ah, all is well!

Distinguishing reality from fantasy

Is It Real?

Introduce your youngsters to a world of fantasy mixed with reality when you share the story of Max's adventure to where the wild things are! To begin, write the word *fantasy* on the board. Ask volunteers to explain what it means, giving examples to support their answers. Also list related words, such as *pretend* and *make-believe.* Next, display the book's cover and read the title. Ask students to study the cover and prompt them to predict whether the story will be about something real or something make-believe. Share the story with the class. Afterward, discuss the accuracy of their predictions. Then ask youngsters to name events in the story that could be real and events that are fantasy. List student responses on a chart similar to the one shown. Keep the chart on display as a reminder about the difference between reality and fantasy.

Real	Fantasy
Max wears a wolf suit.	A forest grows inside Max's bedroom.
Max is acting very wild.	The walls disappear and become the world all around.
Max's mother is angry with him.	Max sails for almost a year and doesn't eat, change, or grow.
Max is sent to his room.	Max tames the wild things with a magic trick.
Max feels lonely without his family.	Max becomes the king of all wild things.
Max's supper is in his room.	

What the Wild Things Do

What makes this story so much fun? It's what those wild things do! Invite each child to act like a wild thing with this movement activity. In advance, write each word or phrase from the list below on an index card. Have students recall when they've ever acted like a wild thing. Ask what they did that made them so wild. Then have students recall how the wild things in the story behave. Encourage them to revisit the book to cite specific examples. Next, review the part of the story where Max sees the wild things for the first time. Ask youngsters to discuss the wild things' actions. Display the prepared word cards and have students read each word aloud.

Lead the group to suggest words that could be added and write them on index cards as well. Gather the cards, and then flash them one at a time as you challenge your youngsters to read the word silently and then perform the matching action. Let the wild rumpus start!

roar
gnash teeth
roll eyes
show claws
be still
bow
jump
swing
march
stop

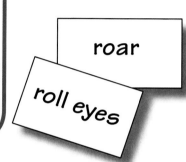

Max in Action

Max's actions are a very important part of this spirited story. Review the book and encourage students to describe the things that Max does. Write each action on a sentence strip. (See the ordered list below for suggestions.) Next, display the strips and ask volunteers to put them in sequential order, using the book as a reference. Then direct each child to select a trio of sequential sentences and write them on a 12" x 18" sheet of construction paper folded to produce three sections as shown. Ask the child to draw and color a picture for each sentence; then have her share her sequence of story scenes with the class. Aren't Max's actions interesting?

Max chases the dog.
Max says, "I'll eat you up!"
Max goes to his room.
Max sees the wild things acting wild!
Max says, "Be still!"
Max tames the wild things.
Max leads the wild rumpus.
Max sends the wild things to bed.

Max chases the dog.

Max says, "I'll eat you up."

Max goes to his room.

King for a Day

Get your youngsters thinking about being king for a day, just like Max, with this art-inspired project. In advance, provide each child with a 12" x 18" sheet of white construction paper, pencil, glue, and a speech bubble cut from writing paper. Also gather a five-inch circle tracer, a plate of yellow tempera paint, and a sponge (cut to resemble a crown shape) for each small group.

Revisit the part of the story when Max is made king of all wild things. Talk about some of the things Max decides to do as the king *(lead a wild rumpus, send the wild things to bed without supper, go home)*. Give the children the opportunity to share what they would do if they were kings for a day.

Afterward, divide students into small groups and provide the materials listed above. Then direct each child to trace a circle on the left-hand side of his paper and draw his face on the circle. Next, have him use the sponge and paint to stamp a crown shape onto the circle. Have each child write on the speech bubble what he would do if he were king for a day and then glue it in place as shown. Provide time for students to share their writings with the class. If desired, post the finished products on a bulletin board titled "If I Were King…"

Making Wild Things

Your youngsters can make their own wild things in this wacky word game! To prepare, copy the word cards on page 34 onto construction paper, cut them apart, and put them in a paper lunch bag. Make three construction paper copies of the body part patterns on page 33. Cut out the patterns and then glue one set to the bag, making a wild thing, as shown. If desired, laminate the other two sets for durability before storing them in a plastic zippered bag.

To play the game, two players take turns pulling word cards from the paper bag without looking. The first player reads his chosen word (using letter-sound association or having the other player help him sound it out if necessary), selects the corresponding body part from the plastic bag, and puts the word card back in the paper bag. If he already has the body part, he returns the card to the paper bag, and his turn is over. Play continues until each child collects an entire set of body parts and is able to assemble a complete wild thing. Oh, those wild, wacky, wonderful words!

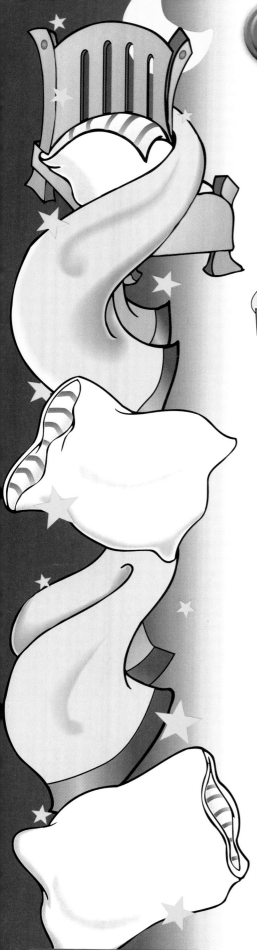

Wild Antics

Encourage your youngsters to share their wild experiences with a writing opportunity they can really sink their claws into! To prepare, gather an oval cutout (paw), three Bugles corn snacks or elongated construction paper triangles (claws), writing paper, and glue for each student. Begin by discussing why Max's mother thinks he is a wild thing. Prompt students to talk about the wild things Max does in the story before being sent to his room. Ask students if they have ever had times when they might have seemed wild to others. Allow time for students to share their experiences with the class. Provide the materials listed above. Direct each child to write about a time when she was a wild thing. Next, ask her to title the paw and then glue it to the top of her paper. Help her glue the claws in place as shown. Encourage students to share their writing with the class. Let the wild antics begin!

> **One Day I Was a Wild Thing**
>
> It was Saturday. I felt like jumping on my bed. I jumped high and low. Then I bumped my nose. It stayed red until Sunday. Sunday I was not wild anymore.
>
> Michelle

A Forest of Writing

Get your youngsters writing about make-believe things with an activity that grows right along with their imaginations! To begin, write the word *imagination* on the board. Ask the children what imagination is, encouraging them to cite specific examples to support their answers. Explain that Max has a lot of imagination, and have students recall examples from the story. Ask students if they have ever imagined or pretended anything. Allow time for them to share their experiences with the class.

To introduce the writing project, provide each child with a giant leaf cutout. Explain that as Max begins to use his imagination, his bedroom walls grow into a forest and that with a little imagination, your classroom walls can too. Direct each child to write (or dictate for you to write) on her leaf shape a sentence about something she has imagined. Display the giant leaves on twisted crepe paper vines, creating a growing forest on the walls of the classroom, similar to Max's walls. Encourage the children to add their imaginative writings from time to time to "grow" the forest. Oh, my! Our classroom is growing a forest too!

> I pretend I am a country singer in a band.
> Kara

hand	body
hand	head
horns	feet
tail	teeth

Seven Blind Mice

Written and illustrated by Ed Young

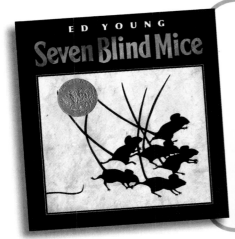

Just what *is* that strange Something by the pond? Tag along with seven blind mice as they attempt to find out exactly what it is. One by one they go, each exploring a different part and identifying the Something as a different thing! Finally, on the seventh day, the white mouse diligently works to look at the entire Something, and in doing so, discovers its true identity. This endearing fable proves that knowing a part is okay, but "wisdom comes from seeing the whole."

Retelling

Flannelboard Fun

Bring Ed Young's book to life on your flannelboard with this long-lasting, interactive display. Ahead of time, gather yarn, seven 4" x 5" scraps of felt (red, green, yellow, purple, orange, blue, and white), and one ten-inch square of gray felt. To prepare, enlarge (at least 200%) the elephant pattern on page 40. Trace its outline onto the gray felt, cut it out, and use a marker to draw on the ear, tusk, and eye. For mice, trace the body and ear patterns (page 40) onto each color of felt. After cutting them out, follow the diagram on page 40 to create the mice for your flannelboard.

After an initial reading of the story, place the elephant on the flannelboard; then give each mouse to a different student. As you read the story again, have the corresponding child place his mouse on the elephant part being investigated. Then have the child move his mouse over to the side to create a stack of mice as shown in the book. Continue until everyone has had a turn to be a mouse. For more fun, make the materials accessible for youngsters to perform retellings on their own!

Everything Is in Order

Get your students thinking about the little details of the story with this independent center that reinforces ordinal number words. To prepare, copy page 39 for each child. Put the pages, a copy of *Seven Blind Mice,* pencils, and crayons in a center. As each child silently rereads the book, have him think about the order in which the mice set out to investigate. Encourage him to pay special attention to the ordinal number words in the story. Next, help him read the directions on the reproducible. Have the child follow the examples to help him complete the rest of the page. Finally, allow time for the student to color the first six mice to match their names. If desired, copy the answer key provided on page 80 for easy self-checking. It's all in the details!

Word Sort

This story provides a wonderful opportunity to practice classifying. In advance, prepare three sentence strips, labeling one "Ordinal Numbers," one "Days of the Week," and one "Color Words." Place them side by side in the top row of a pocket chart and set it aside. Then program 21 large index cards, each with a different color, day of the week, or ordinal number word from the story. To begin, provide each student (or pair of students) with a word card. Challenge the class to sort themselves into groups. Guide students to conclude that there are three main groups. Then invite the members of each group to sit together on the floor.

Ask students which ordinal word comes first *(first).* Invite the student with this card to come forward and place it in the pocket chart below its corresponding heading. Next, ask students if they remember the day of the week the story mentions first *(Monday).* Invite that child to bring his card forward and place it under its

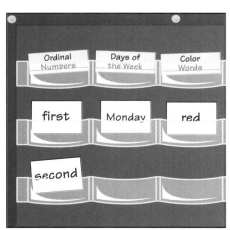

corresponding heading. Then ask which mouse ventured out first *(red).* Again, have that child come forward and place his card below its corresponding heading. Continue in this manner, using the book as a reference if necessary. Finally, have the class chorally read each list vertically to help reinforce ordinal words. Your students will quickly have it all sorted out!

Can You See It?

Help your youngsters take a closer look at everyday objects as they complete this visual exercise. Remind students that in this story, the green mouse thinks the elephant is a snake. Call on a volunteer to explain why as you show students the illustration. *(Green Mouse only sees the elephant's curled trunk.)* Have students discuss the word *snake* and describe what snakes look like, and what snakes do. Next, encourage students to visualize other things that look like a snake. Create a list on the board as students offer suggestions. Continue in this same manner as you discuss pillars, spears, cliffs, fans, and ropes.

Provide each student with a sheet of drawing paper. Have her choose one of the items listed that could resemble an object mentioned in the story. Then direct her to draw a picture of both items and write about how the two things are visually similar. Provide time for each child to share her work with the class. I can see it! Can you?

A wet paintbrush looks like a tiny spear.

I think a fan looks like a big slice of pizza.

Simply Similes

Give your students a chance to create comparisons, just like White Mouse does with this similes activity. Ahead of time, gather several nonfiction references about elephants. To begin, review the page in the story where the seventh mouse uses similes to describe the elephant. As you read each simile, have youngsters repeat the descriptive words *(sturdy, supple, wide, sharp, breezy, stringy)*. Display the reference books. Encourage students to explore the pictures and text as they brainstorm a list of words to describe an elephant's size, color, strength, and appearance. (See the list for suggestions.)

Write the incomplete sentence below on the board. Give each child a sheet of construction paper. Have her write the sentence and fill in the blanks with an adjective and an associated object of her choice, using the brainstormed list as a reference if necessary. Finally, have her illustrate her sentence and share it with the class. Yippee for similes!

The elephant is as __tall__ as a __tree__ .

Kaleigh

round
bumpy
gray
wrinkled
big
strong

Seeing Things Differently

The mice certainly see things differently when it comes to identifying the Something in this story! Explore different viewpoints with this creative-writing activity. Begin by having students discuss their views about specific things, such as games to play during recess, favorite cartoons, or favorite foods. Talk about how one person's views can differ from someone else's. Lead students to conclude that it is okay to see things differently.

Provide each student with a copy of the glasses pattern on page 40. Have him think of someone who disagrees with him about something. Have him fill in the blank on the left side of the pattern with the person's name and write about that person's opinion. Then, on the right side, have him write his opinion regarding the same issue. Direct him to title the tag with his topic and color his pattern before cutting it along the bold lines.

If desired, post the finished products on a bulletin board titled "We See Things Differently."

The Way We See Food — My brother **thinks** pizza is the best food in the world. | **I think** the best food in the world is chicken.

Take a Closer Look

This unique writing activity will give your students a fresh perspective about how things aren't always as they seem. Ahead of time, obtain a picture map of an area with many different parts, such as an amusement park, zoo, or museum. To prepare the map, cut it into enough pieces to give each student one piece. (Be sure that each piece has one picture of an attraction, exhibit, etc.)

To begin the activity, give each student a piece of the map. Tell each student that he is going on a field trip to the place pictured on his paper. After he has identified his destination, direct him to write about how he would feel going there on a field trip. Allow students to share their work and opinions with the class.

Afterward, invite each child to bring his piece forward as you tape the map back together. Now, as students view the map in its entirety, discuss how their opinions of the field trip might have been different had they known about all the other areas in the map. Remind students that it wasn't until the seventh mouse looked at the Something in its entirety that he correctly identified it. Lead students to conclude that things are not always as they seem at first glance—"wisdom comes from seeing the whole."

Going on a field trip to a roller coaster would be great! I would ride it all day long!

Patricia

ROLLER COASTER ZONE

Name _____

Line 'em Up!

Read the first sentence below.
Trace the **ordinal** word.
Then trace the color word to match.
Fill in the remaining blanks in order.
Use the word bank to help you.

The _____first_____ mouse was _____red_____.

The _____second_____ mouse was _____.

The _____ mouse was _____.

The _____ mouse was _____.

The _____ mouse was _____.

The _____ mouse was _____.

The _____ mouse was _____.

Color the mice to match their names.

Word Bank

| fourth | second | seventh | first | fifth | third | sixth |

Note to the teacher: Use with "Everything Is in Order" on page 36.

Elephant and Mouse Patterns
Use with "Flannelboard Fun" on page 35.

Glasses Pattern
Use with "Seeing Things Differently" on page 38.

elephant

mouse ear

I think

mouse
body

thinks

1. Place a piece of yarn in the fold before gluing closed.
2. Glue on the ear and draw an eye and nose with a marker.

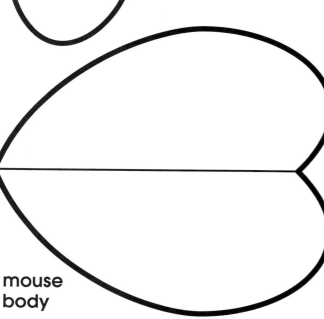

The Way We See

The Cat in the Hat

Written and illustrated by Dr. Seuss

In this story, two children are faced with staying indoors on a cold, rainy day while their mother is out. Enter the Cat in the Hat! He arrives prepared with tricks and games of all kinds that end up making more of a mess than anything else. Their tidy house is quickly turned upside down and even the fish cannot keep order. As their mother is about to return, the Cat in the Hat performs his best trick of all—just in the nick of time!

Listening for a purpose

A Difference in Character

There's no doubt about it, the fish and cat do not see eye to eye! In this prereading activity, students will explore the personalities of these two characters while improving their listening skills. Before reading, display the book's cover and read the title. Discuss what the children already know and can recall about the story. Next, divide the class into two groups. Assign one group to pay special attention to the actions and expressions of the cat, and the other group to pay special attention to the actions and expressions of the fish. Then read the story. Afterward, have the children who focused on the cat talk about his mischievous, carefree personality. Also allow time for the other group to share its opinions about the anxiousness and uneasiness of the fish. Lead children to conclude that the concerns of the fish and the total lack of concern of the cat help make this story fun and exciting.

Before and After

Help your students keep track of every event in the story with this hands-on sequencing activity. In advance, make a construction paper copy of the sentence cards on page 45. Also gather 12 similarly sized white strips. Place the cards and strips at the front of the room.

Remind students that the events in a story occur in a logical order. This helps the reader easily follow what is happening. Explain to students that an event from *The Cat in the Hat* is written on each strip. Then tape the card with the first event to the board and read it together. Next, call on a volunteer to tell what happened *before* the event. After confirming her answer with the book, write the "before" event on a blank strip and tape it to the left of the first event. Then call on another volunteer to tell what happened *after* the event. Write it on a blank strip and tape it to the right of the first event. Repeat this process with the remaining strips to show the complete story in sequential order. For a future review of the story, number the backs of the strips to show their order, mix them up, and have students reorder them. Students can just flip the strips to check their work!

| The children sit inside with nothing to do. | Something goes bump! | The Cat in the Hat arrives. |

Fishing for a Rhyme

It's rhyme time, and who knows rhyming better than Dr. Seuss? Your students will after they polish their rhyming skills at this center. Ahead of time, gather five white paper lunch bags. Draw a fishbowl outline on each bag and label them as shown. Next, make a construction paper copy of the fish cards on page 46 and then cut them apart. Also make a copy of the answer key on page 80. Place the cards, bags, answer key, and a Cat in the Hat stuffed toy (if available) at a center.

To complete the center, a student reads the word on any card and then places it in the bag labeled with its rhyming word. Direct him to continue in this manner with the remaining cards. Afterward, have the student empty each bag, one at a time, and check his answers using the answer key. Now that's a bowl full of fun!

Cat Characteristics

That cat sure does have a personality! Have students take a closer look at his qualities with this adorable graphic organizer. After rereading and discussing the book, draw a simple cat face on the board similar to the one shown. Lead students in a discussion about what they know about the cat after reading the story. Talk about what he is like based on his actions. Call on a student volunteer to offer a descriptive word about the cat. Write it on a whisker. Direct the student to tell why she thinks the cat has that trait and offer an example from the story to support her answer. Continue in the same manner with each remaining trait. Afterward, prompt students to think of

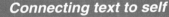

other story characters who are similar to the Cat in the Hat. Encourage them to name the trait each character shares with the cat and give a reason for their choice. What an unforgettable character!

What Would You Do?

Students can help point Sally and her brother in the "write" direction with this letter-writing activity! At the end of the story, the brother asks, "What would you do if your mother asked you?" Discuss with students what they think the children in the story should do. Then, after a quick review of the parts of a friendly letter, direct each student to write Sally and her brother, telling them what they should say to their mother and why. Give each child an opportunity to read his letter aloud. To conclude the activity, mention the silly nature of this book and that in reality, strangers are never allowed in our homes when parents aren't there. Also discuss the importance of keeping parents (or other guardians) informed about everything that happens. Write on!

Dear Kids,
  I think you should tell your mom the truth. Moms find out everything anyway. If you don't tell her and she finds out, she will be mad. Make sure you tell her right away, before the fish does!
        Your Friend,
          John

A Better Box of Fun

When the cat decides to show the children a new game, who could know that it would lead to such a mess? Get your students thinking about positive alternatives to Fun-in-a-Box with this writing activity. To begin, remind students that when the Cat in the Hat decides to play another good game, it causes more *trouble* than fun! Have students brainstorm several more appropriate indoor games. Then give each child a half sheet of paper. Direct her to fold her paper in half to create a box shape. Next, have the child choose an indoor game from the brainstormed list (or select one of her own) and write several descriptive sentences about it on the inside of the box. After labeling and coloring the outside of the box, allow time for each child to share her work with the class. If desired, save the boxes and use them to choose games on rainy recess days!

When I have to stay indoors, I like to play checkers. My friend Kathy comes to my house. I like to be the red team. Kathy is good at double jumping. She wins a lot.

How Do You Feel?

The Cat in the Hat offers a unique opportunity to discuss feelings and how they can change in different situations. Give your students a chance to identify with the children's changing feelings and relate them to their own lives. Begin by asking the children how the boy and girl in the story may feel at different times. Guide students to use the illustrations in the book to support their answers. Help students discover that the children are bored, surprised, speechless, afraid, determined, and glad. Help students describe each feeling and share any personal experiences they have had involving these feelings. Next, have each child choose one feeling and write about the event in the story that causes it. Also have him write about a time when he felt that way. Encourage him to be as descriptive as possible in his writing. Provide each student with a sheet of construction paper. Have him draw hands and a face portraying his chosen feeling to attach to his paper before taking it home for more sharing.

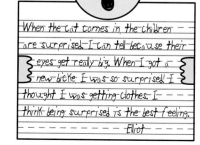

When the cat comes in, the children are surprised. I can tell because their eyes get really big. When I got a new bike, I was so surprised! I thought I was getting clothes. I think being surprised is the best feeling.
— Elliot

Something goes bump!

The cat says he'll show them some tricks.

The cat stands on the ball.

The cat opens the box.

The Things run down the hall.

The cat cleans up the mess.

Fish Cards

Use with "Fishing for a Rhyme" on page 42.

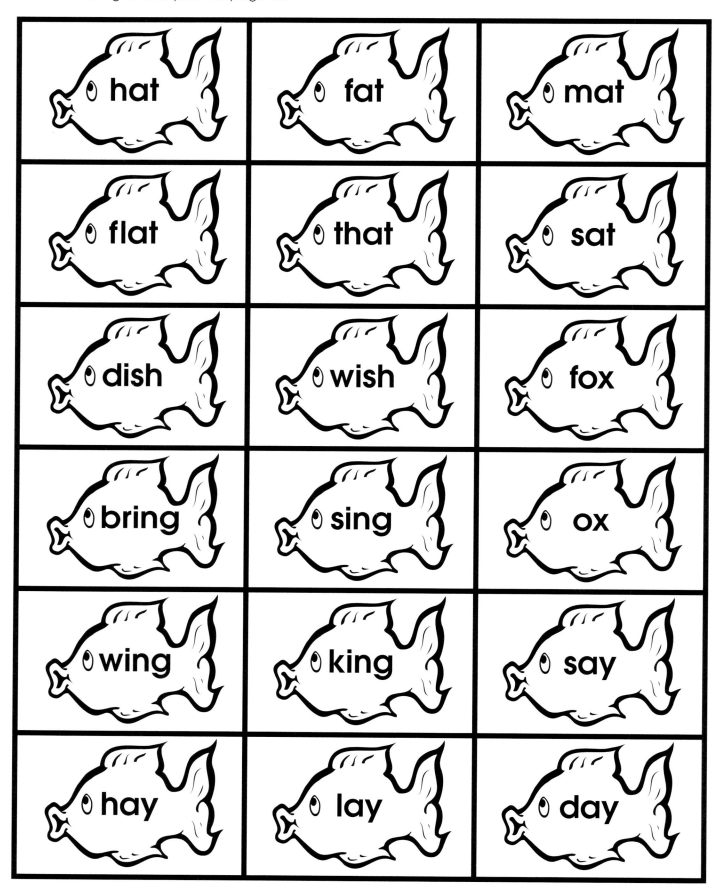

hat | fat | mat

flat | that | sat

dish | wish | fox

bring | sing | ox

wing | king | say

hay | lay | day

Harry the Dirty Dog

Written by Gene Zion
Illustrated by Margaret Bloy Graham

Harry hates baths so much that he decides to hide the scrubbing brush and run away! After an afternoon of playing, he soon wonders if his family misses him and decides to go home. However, Harry is so dirty that his family doesn't recognize him. Harry tries to convince them by doing his old tricks, but to no avail. Just when he is about to give up, he remembers the scrubbing brush. Harry digs it up and heads straight for the bathtub. Once the children start bathing him, they discover that it is indeed Harry. This is one time that Harry is thankful for a little soap and water!

HARRY
THE DIRTY DOG
by Gene Zion
pictures by Margaret Bloy Graham

Connecting text to self

How Harry Feels

A lot happens to Harry in one day! Use this discussion activity to give students an opportunity to relate to Harry's feelings. After reading the book, discuss the story's events with your students and make a list of all the different feelings Harry probably experienced. (See the list for suggestions.) Then invite your youngsters to share any personal experiences they've had with these emotions. Also talk about how students relate to the way Harry feels about getting dirty while playing and taking baths. Your youngsters will have no trouble relating to the many changing feelings of this lovable character!

Events	Feelings
Harry runs away.	brave
Harry plays tag.	friendly
Harry gets dirty.	excited
Harry thinks of his family.	lonely
Harry's family doesn't recognize him.	hopeful
Harry gets a bath.	happy
Harry's family is happy that he is home.	relieved
Harry goes to sleep.	relaxed

Delightfully Dirty

Get down and dirty with this cute two-day project as students recall details from the story. On the first day, divide students into small groups and provide each group with a paper plate of brown paint and a sheet of white paper. Direct each child to make a handprint of one hand on her paper. After the paint dries, instruct the student to cut out her handprint and set it aside.

On the second day, reread *Harry the Dirty Dog* to students. Help them recall the different ways that Harry gets dirty. Then give each child a sheet of story paper and direct her to write about and illustrate her favorite messy activity. To finish, have her use a black marker to write her name on her premade handprint. Mount each child's handprint and story on a bulletin board titled "How We Get Dirty."

Let's See Some Action!

Take advantage of all the activity in this story with this dramatic-play idea! To begin, program a supply of index cards, each with a different action word from the story. (See the list below.) Then gather your students together for a game of charades. Remind students that in the story Harry does many things. Have students brainstorm a quick list of the things he does. Then show students the cards and tell them that written on each one is an action Harry performs. To play, invite one child to pick a word card. Help him identify the word; then have him pretend to be Harry and act it out. Instruct the rest of the group to guess the action word being depicted. Designate the child who guesses correctly as the next actor. Continue for several rounds or as long as time allows. If desired, make a simple pair of dog ears to attach to a headband for students to wear and encourage them to really get into character!

jump	dance
bury	sing
walk	dig
sit	crawl
run	wag
carry	slide
roll	bark
dash	beg
play dead	sleep

What Happened Next?

Set the story straight and work on students' recall abilities during this group chain game. Before beginning, reread *Harry the Dirty Dog* to students. Next, provide each student with a copy of the cards on page 51. Have him draw a picture on each card showing Harry performing the action described in the sentence. Allow time for him to color and cut out the picture cards and then place them in order on a 4" x 18" strip of construction paper. Check students' work before having them glue their pictures in place. Allow them to keep their papers to use as a reference during the game if needed.

To play, name an event from the story and then call out "before" or "after." A student volunteer calls out a story event that matches your description and then says "before" or "after" to keep the game going. Continue in this manner until everyone has had a turn. How waggingly wonderful!

Harry is burying the scrubbing brush in the yard. / *Harry is playing tag with the other dogs.* / *Harry is sliding down the coal chute.* / *Harry is rolling over.* / *Harry's family is giving him a bath.* / *Harry is sleeping on his bed.* / John

Harry Likes...

We know Harry doesn't like taking a bath, but what *does* he like? This writing activity is sure to generate many possibilities! Tell children that it is very clear in the story that Harry hates baths. Pair students and direct them to list things Harry may like, such as playing Frisbee or swimming. Allow time for each pair to share its ideas with the class. Next, provide each student with a sheet of story paper. Direct him to write a detailed paragraph about something that Harry really enjoys and why he likes it so much. Allow time for him to illustrate his work before sharing it with the class. Write on!

For Your Own Good

Find out what makes your little ones want to run and hide, just like Harry, with this writing activity. Remind students that Harry dislikes baths so much that he decides to run away. Encourage them to think about why Harry's family would make him do something he does not enjoy. *(They want to take good care of him.)* Invite students to brainstorm other things Harry's family may make him do that he does not enjoy. For example, his family makes him eat dog food instead of people food because it's healthier for him. Discuss how this relates to students' lives in that their parents make them eat a balanced meal instead of junk food all the time. Help them conclude that although parents require kids to do certain things they may not always like, it is usually for a good reason. Next, direct each child to write about something her parent or guardian makes her do that she doesn't enjoy but is for a good reason. Encourage students to write about how these things could benefit them or possibly make them more responsible. Allow time for students to share their work with the class. See, it's not so bad!

Harry's Adventures

This journal-writing center is a great way for students to gain a different perspective of the story. Ahead of time, copy the journal pattern on page 52 to make a class supply. Cut the patterns apart and place them at a center along with several pencils, erasers, scissors, a black fine-tip marker, and a black ink pad. In turn, send each student to the center. Direct her to write a journal entry as if she were Harry about an exciting adventure he is taking. Next, have the child use her index finger, the ink pad, and the marker to make pawprints along the border as shown. Finally, have her cut the entry out along the bold lines. If desired, bind the completed pages into a mini booklet titled "Adventures With Harry" and place it in your classroom library. Harry, you lucky dog!

Date _____ March 7, 2003

I am on an exciting adventure

in the jungle. The animals and I

like to climb trees, swing from

the vines, and slide down the

branches. I get very dirty!

Harry

©The Education Center, Inc. • *Reading & Writing With Picture Books* • TEC1790

Harry's family is giving him a bath.

Harry is burying the scrubbing brush in the yard.

Harry is rolling over.

Harry is sliding down the coal chute.

Harry is sleeping on his bed.

Harry is playing tag with the other dogs.

Journal Patterns

Use with "Harry's Adventures" on page 50.

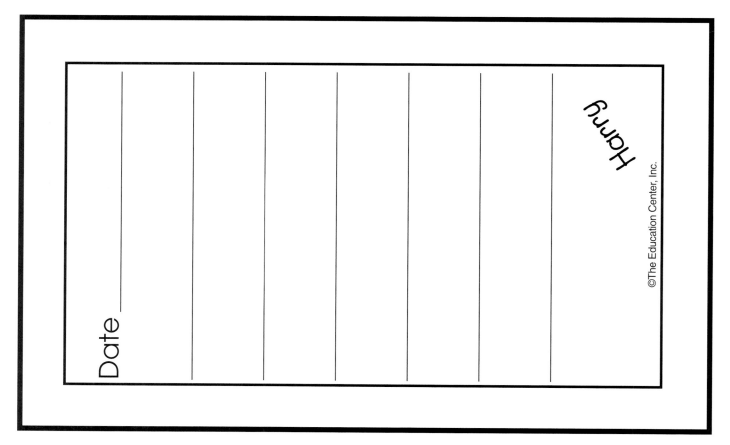

Zomo the Rabbit:
A Trickster Tale From West Africa

Written and illustrated by Gerald McDermott

In this West African tale, we meet Zomo, a mischievous young rabbit who is not big or strong, but he is very clever. Zomo wants more; he wants wisdom. He goes to Sky God asking for wisdom. Sky God gives Zomo three impossible tasks to accomplish in order to earn the wisdom he desires. The rabbit uses his wit to successfully outsmart a fish, cow, and leopard and is granted wisdom. However, in the end, Zomo realizes that it is speed, not wisdom, that he will depend on in order to avoid the animals' revenge!

Sequencing

Get the Story Straight

This concentration game is a fun way for pairs to work together on sequencing skills. Provide each pair of students with a construction paper copy of the game cards on page 57. Direct the pair to cut out its cards and spread them out facedown. To play the game, Player 1 flips over two cards to try to match a pictured event with the sentence describing it. If the student makes a match, direct him to keep both cards. If he does not make a match, direct him to turn the cards back over. Then Player 2 takes a turn. Play continues until all matches have been made. Next, have the pair arrange all of the cards faceup. Have the pair work together to put the events and sentences in sequential order. Encourage students to refer to the book as a reference. What a sequencing sensation!

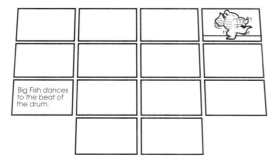

He's Like Me

Give your youngsters the opportunity to take a closer look at Gerald McDermott's intriguing characters and they'll be surprised to see how much they have in common! To prepare, program each of five large index cards with a different character's name from the story *(Zomo, Sky God, Big Fish, Wild Cow, and Leopard)*. Reread the story. Display the name cards and then write on the board a different word to describe each character. (See the list below for suggestions.) Challenge students to tape a name card beside the word that best describes that character. Accept and discuss all reasonable answers. Next, discuss how the characteristics of the animals have played a part in students' lives and allow time for them to share their stories with the class. By relating to personal experiences, students will better understand the story's interesting characters.

clever
powerful
embarrassed
mad
clumsy

The fish is embarrassed. He's like me because one time I fell down on the playground and I was embarrassed.

A Rabbit Trick

Build cause-and-effect relationships with an activity that's as easy as pulling a rabbit out of a hat! To prepare, use the rabbit pattern on page 58 to make six cutouts. Program each cutout with a different story event from the list below. Place the rabbits in a hat. Talk to students about the difference between cause and effect. Tell students that there are many cause-and-effect relationships in *Zomo the Rabbit.* Then direct their attention to the hat filled with rabbits. To begin, direct a student to pull a rabbit from the hat. Help him read the event aloud and then tell the cause of the event, using the book to support his answer. Continue with other students until all of the rabbits have been chosen. Ta-da!

Events
- Zomo visits Sky God.
- Big Fish's scales fall off.
- Wild Cow gets her horns stuck in the palm tree.
- Leopard's tooth falls out.
- Sky God gives Zomo wisdom.
- Zomo has to run very, very fast.

Wisdom in My World

Find out who your students think is the wisest of all with this card-making activity. In advance, make a construction paper copy of the owl pattern on page 58 for each student. Begin by asking students what they think *wisdom* means and list their responses on the board. Lead students to conclude that *wisdom* means "knowledge" and that a person who is wise understands many things and uses good judgment. Remind students that in the story, Zomo desires wisdom. Ask students whether they think Zomo is wise and why. Encourage them to cite examples from the story and talk about how Zomo uses his knowledge to accomplish each task. Next, ask each student to name someone in his life who he feels is wise and tell why. Give each child an owl pattern and direct him to personalize it and then cut it out. Next, have him glue his owl onto the front of a folded sheet of paper. Then, on the inside of his card, have him write why he thinks that person is wise. What a nice surprise it will be when these special cards are delivered!

Whooo Is the
Wisest of All?
You! That's Whooo!

To Uncle Chuck

From Ian

I think you are very wise. You know all about the world. You visit really interesting places. You teach me about Spain and Mexico. Thank you for sharing your wisdom with me.
Love,
Ian

Tricking the Trickster

See how creative your students can be when you give them a chance to turn the tables on the trickster! To begin, discuss how Big Fish, Wild Cow, and Leopard are outsmarted by Zomo. Talk about different things each character could do to avoid being tricked.

Then provide each student with a sheet of story paper. Have each student imagine himself as either the fish, cow, or leopard and write about what he would do differently to avoid being tricked. Encourage him to include complete, detailed sentences in his writing. Then have the child illustrate his paragraph. Finally, allow time for students to share their stories with the class. Look out, Zomo!

If I were the fish, I wouldn't dance so fast. I would dance slowly to Zomo's music. That way I could dance as long as I want. Zomo wouldn't get my scales then! Jamie

Zomo's New Adventures

Give your students a chance to set a new task for Zomo to accomplish with this creative-writing activity. In advance, gather a sheet of writing paper, various scraps of construction paper, scissors, a large cotton ball, crayons, and glue for each child. Remind students that Zomo has to earn the wisdom he desires. Write "earn" on the board and ask students what it means. Next, poll your youngsters to see whether they think it is easy or difficult for Zomo to earn wisdom. Then brainstorm other tasks Sky God could ask Zomo to do, and write them on the board. Provide students with the materials listed above. Next, have each student choose a new task for Zomo. Students may select one from the brainstormed list or think of their own. Then have each student write a creative story on the writing paper telling how Zomo might accomplish the task. To accent her writing, have each student draw a rabbit head and ears on construction paper and cut them out. After she adds colorful details to the rabbit, guide the student to glue the ears onto the head and attach the head and tail to her paper as shown. Allow time for student volunteers to share their stories with the class. Let the adventures begin!

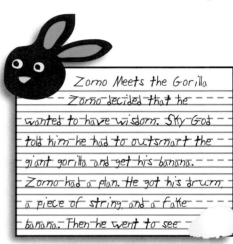

Zomo Meets the Gorilla
  Zomo decided that he
wanted to have wisdom. Sky God
told him he had to outsmart the
giant gorilla and get his banana.
Zomo had a plan. He got his drum,
a piece of string, and a fake
banana. Then he went to see

A Penny for Your Thoughts

Try this partner game for a great review of fact and opinion! To prepare, draw a large gameboard grid with 16 boxes. Write a sentence from below in each box. Then make two copies of the grid. Next, cut apart the boxes from one copy to make answer cards. Program the back of each card with "F" or "O" so students can check each other's answers during the game. Place the grid, answer cards, and 16 pennies at a center.

Before a pair of students begins the game, have each child choose to mark his correctly answered spaces with heads or tails. To play, Player 1 chooses a box from the grid, reads the statement, and declares it fact or opinion. Then Player 2 checks the matching answer card to confirm the answer. If Player 1 has answered correctly, he marks the box with a penny. If he answers incorrectly, Player 2 takes a turn. The first player to have four boxes in a row (or the most boxes) wins.

Facts	Opinions
• Zomo is a rabbit.	• Wisdom is easy to earn.
• Sky God grants Zomo wisdom.	• Zomo tries hard.
• Zomo wants wisdom.	• Zomo plays beautiful music on his drum.
• Big Fish has scales.	• Big Fish is a good dancer.
• Leopard loses a tooth.	• The palm tree is very big.
• Zomo plays his drum.	• Wild Cow's milk is delicious.
• Wild Cow gets angry.	• The rock is heavy.
• Leopard rolls down the hill.	• Sky God is nice.

Wild Cow gets her horns stuck in the tree.	The animals are chasing after Zomo.	Big Fish dances to the beat of the drum.
Zomo takes the scales, milk, and tooth to Sky God.	Big Fish's scales fall off.	Leopard rolls down the hill.
Sky God gives Zomo three tasks.		

Rabbit Pattern
Use with "A Rabbit Trick" on page 54.

©The Education Center, Inc.

Owl Pattern
Use with "Wisdom in My World" on page 55.

Whooo Is the
Wisest of All?
You! That's Whooo!

To: _____

From: _____

©The Education Center, Inc.

©The Education Center, Inc. • *Reading & Writing With Picture Books* • TEC1790

Miss Nelson Is Missing!

Written by Harry Allard
Illustrated by James Marshall

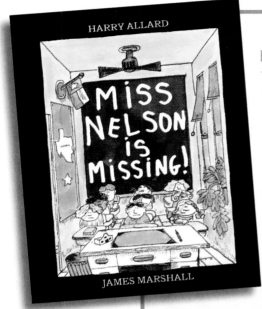

HARRY ALLARD

MISS NELSON IS MISSING!

JAMES MARSHALL

The kids in Room 207 just won't behave! They're rude, disrespectful, and stubborn—so much so that their teacher, Miss Nelson, employs the help of her secret friend, Miss Viola Swamp. Miss Swamp's mean, no-nonsense approach quickly gets the students' attention. Very soon the children realize the benefit of having Miss Nelson, and they long to get her back. Some even go to the police for help, but to no avail. As the students settle in for yet another day of Miss Swamp's discipline, they are surprised and delighted to hear Miss Nelson's sweet voice instead. And from that point on, Miss Nelson doesn't have another minute's trouble!

Activating prior knowledge

Classroom Etiquette

There's no doubt about it. Miss Nelson's class is in dire need of a lesson in etiquette! Use this prereading activity to remind students about appropriate classroom conduct. To begin, talk with students about what they feel is acceptable classroom behavior. Encourage them to offer specific examples for their suggestions. Then read the story aloud to students. Discuss with children how they feel about the students' behavior at the beginning of the story. Revisit the illustrations on the first three pages and have students comment on how they think the class's behavior makes Miss Nelson feel. Then compare it to the students' behavior at the end of the story and the positive change that takes place. Next, brainstorm with students rules for classroom etiquette, listing each suggestion on chart paper. As a class, discuss the significance of each one and the importance of maintaining a positive atmosphere in the classroom. Display the rules and encourage students to review them daily. What a proper way to start the day!

> **Rules of Etiquette for Room 2B**
> Do your best work.
> Be responsible for yourself.
> Respect others.

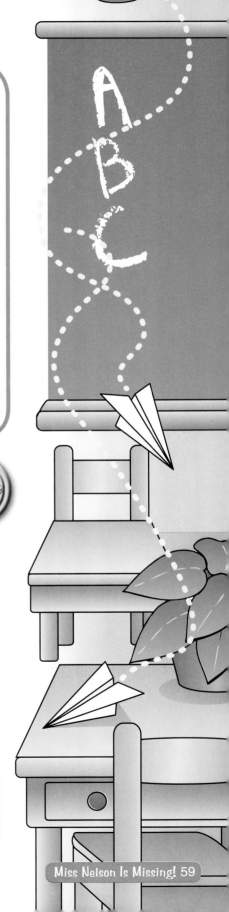

She's Not So Bad

The children in Room 207 are surprised to find that their substitute teacher is not as sweet as Miss Nelson. Show your students that Miss Viola Swamp isn't all that bad with this book discussion. To begin, revisit the book's illustrations and discuss the differences in appearance between Miss Nelson and Miss Viola Swamp. Also talk about their different styles of teaching, using the text as a reference. Ask students who they think is the better teacher and why. Lead students to conclude that both teachers have positive qualities. For example, Miss Nelson has a more pleasant personality and the students like her better, but it is Miss Swamp who was able to get the students to behave themselves and complete their work. To provide further practice with comparing and contrasting, have each student complete a copy of "Quite a Character!" on page 63. Students will quickly see that someone who combines fun and hard work makes for the best teacher of all!

It's All in the Name

Get your youngsters thinking about the meaning of names with this creative-writing activity. Ask students how they think Miss Viola Swamp got her name. Help them arrive at a conclusion by discussing the meaning of *swamp* as it relates to the character in the story. Then show students her full-page picture in the book. Next, provide each student with a 9" x 24" piece of white bulletin board paper. Direct her to draw Miss Viola Swamp's striped sock and shoe (similar to the one shown) and then write on the stripes how she thinks she got her name. Have each student color and cut out her drawing; then post the drawings along the hallway for everyone to enjoy. If desired, obtain a name origins reference book and encourage each student to look up the meaning of her own name!

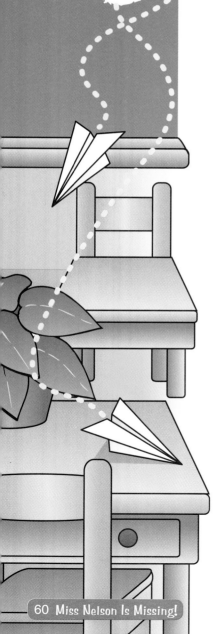

I think Miss Viola Swamp got her name because she's not nice. A swamp is not a nice place. It's dark and dreary. You would not want to spend the day at a swamp or with Viola!

A Contrast in Character

It's a fact—the two teachers in this story are as different as night and day! Invite students to piece together the many other differences from the story while reviewing opposites with this hands-on center. In advance, copy and cut out the cards on page 64. Program the back of each pair of opposites with matching symbols. Store the cards in a plastic resealable bag and place them at a center. To use the center, a child matches a pair of opposite word cards and continues in this manner until all pairs have been matched. To check his work, he simply flips the cards. These opposites are sure to attract a lot of attention from your students!

Please Come Back!

Find out what your students would do to get Miss Nelson back with this letter-writing activity. Have each child pretend that she is in Miss Nelson's class and is faced with having Miss Viola Swamp for the rest of the year—*unless* she can convince Miss Nelson to change her mind. After a quick review of the parts of a friendly letter, instruct each student to write Miss Nelson, asking her to come back. Encourage students to describe what great things she can expect from the class when she returns. Allow time for children to share their letters. If desired, post them on a bulletin board titled "Please Come Back!"

> February 5, 2003
>
> Dear Miss Nelson,
>
> Please come back! We promise not to throw paper planes or make spitballs anymore. We will do our best work. We miss you.
>
> Love,
>
> Kelly

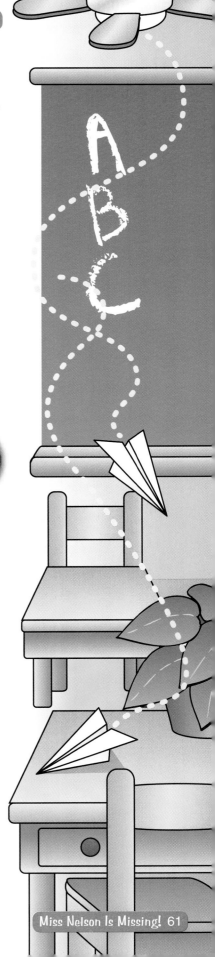

Order in the Classroom

Give students the opportunity to spotlight their sequencing skills with this interactive activity! In advance, program a class supply of paper plates each with a different event from the story. (See the list below for suggestions.) Hole-punch the top of each plate and thread a 24-inch piece of yarn through each hole. Knot the yarn to make a large loop.

Reread the story to students. Then ask them to recall, in no particular order, as many events from the story as possible. For each suggestion, display the paper plate with the matching event until all of them have been suggested. Next, give each student a plate and direct him to hang it around his neck. Then ask students to recall the first event in the story. *(The kids throw paper airplanes.)* Direct the student wearing the appropriately programmed plate to come forward. Then ask students to recall the second event in the story. *(The kids whisper and giggle.)* Direct that child to come forward and link arms with the first student. Continue in this same manner with the remaining events until a class-size chain is made showing all the events in sequential order. What a sequencing sensation!

1. The kids throw paper airplanes.
2. The kids whisper and giggle.
3. The children squirm and make faces.
4. The children are rude during story hour.
5. The kids refuse to do their lessons.
6. Miss Viola Swamp comes to school.
7. The children have a lot of homework.
8. There is no story hour.
9. The children have to sit perfectly still.
10. The kids miss Miss Nelson.
11. Some children go to the police for help.
12. Detective McSmogg says Miss Nelson must be missing.
13. Some kids go to Miss Nelson's house to look for her.
14. Someone thinks Miss Nelson has been eaten by a shark.
15. Someone thinks Miss Nelson has gone to Mars.
16. Someone thinks Miss Nelson's car has been carried off by butterflies.
17. The children hear a sweet voice.
18. The children behave during story hour.
19. Miss Nelson hangs her coat next to a black dress.
20. Detective McSmogg has a new case.

Wish You Were Here!

Where did Miss Nelson *really* go while Miss Viola Swamp was the teacher? Capture your students' imaginations with this postcard-writing activity. To begin, provide each child with a copy of the post-card pattern on page 64. Instruct each student to write a postcard to the class from Miss Nelson. Have the student tell about the place where Miss Nelson has gone and what she is doing there. Then provide time for each child to illustrate Miss Nelson's adventure on the front of the postcard. Where on earth could she be?

Quite a Character!

Cut out the pictures below.
Read each sentence.
Think about the teacher that it describes.
Glue the picture of her dress on the box.

1. I have an unpleasant voice.

2. My students make spitballs.

3. I have a sweet voice.

4. I do not have story hour.

5. I give a lot of homework.

6. My students whisper and giggle.

7. My students do not do their work.

8. I wear an ugly black dress.

Bonus Box: On the back of this sheet, write three words to describe Miss Nelson and three words to describe Miss Viola Swamp.

 Miss Swamp
 Miss Swamp
 Miss Swamp
 Miss Swamp
 Miss Nelson
 Miss Nelson
 Miss Nelson
 Miss Nelson

Note to the teacher: Use this page with "She's Not So Bad" on page 60.

Opposite Cards

Use with "A Contrast in Character" on page 61.

quiet / loud   ugly / pretty

unpleasant / sweet   nice / mean

rude / polite   missing / found

Postcard Pattern

Use with "Wish You Were Here!" on page 62.

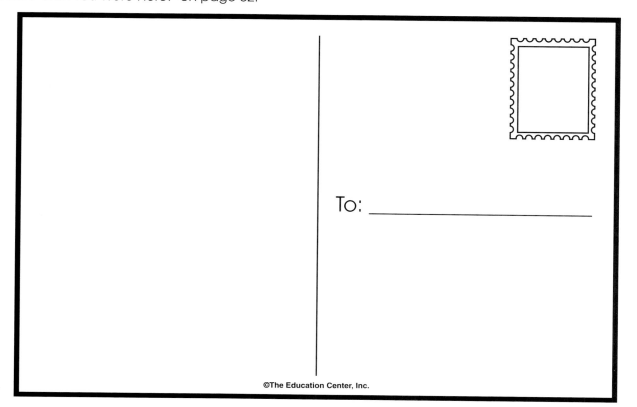

To: _____

©The Education Center, Inc.

Officer Buckle and Gloria

Written and illustrated by Peggy Rathmann

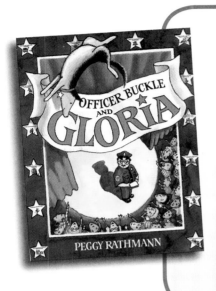

When it comes to safety, Officer Buckle knows his stuff. Unfortunately, his safety speech is quite dry and the young audience quickly loses interest. But then Gloria, the new police dog, arrives on the scene! Unbeknownst to Officer Buckle, Gloria hysterically dramatizes each of his safety tips. Soon lots of schools are requesting Officer Buckle's program—with Gloria, of course! The story takes an unexpected turn when the officer realizes he's been upstaged by his canine partner and discontinues his speaking engagements. It takes Napville School's biggest accident ever to convince him to join Gloria in resuming their showstopping safety tour.

Listening for a purpose

Colorful Characters

If you want your children to listen intently as you read, give them a special job to do. Introduce this story by showing the book's cover. Find out what children see in the cover illustration and ask them to predict what the story is about. Guide them to also contemplate who is in the story and where the story takes place. Then, before you begin reading, give the children specific tasks to accomplish as they listen to the story. Have some children pay special attention to Officer Buckle, some pay special attention to Gloria, and a few others pay particular attention to the children and principal. Since the illustrations carry so much of the meaning in this book, take care to position yourself for reading so that every child can get a good look at each illustration. Pause occasionally to allow children to enjoy Gloria's onstage antics. After reading the book, discuss it with the children. Encourage them to make specific observations about the characters they focused on.

#10 Don't run with SCISSORS in your hand.

#12 Don't play with MATCHES.

#1? Don't play with SPRAY CANS.

#18 Don't leave TENNIS BALLS on the STAIRS.

#21 Don't put ANYTHING in your EAR.

#10
Don't run with CISSORS in your hand.

#12
Don't play with MATCHES.

#15
Don't play with SPRAY CANS.

#18
Don't leave TENNIS BALLS on the STAIRS.

#21
Don't put ANYTHING in your EAR.

What's So Funny?

With all the grins and giggles, few of your students will realize this activity reinforces an important reading strategy—inference. First, without displaying the book, read aloud just the tips that Officer Buckle reads from the stage. Then read the tips while showing the associated illustrations. As children giggle at Gloria's antics in the illustrations, pretend to be puzzled. Ask why they think the tips are funny. Once you've heard students' explanations for the hilarity, explain that there are times when you must look at the pictures to find out what the author wants you to know. In this book, the pictures help readers understand more than what the words are specifically telling.

Reread the safety tips while sharing the illustrations. Have children take turns inferring the chain of events each picture represents. Continue having children infer while discussing the illustrations of Officer Buckle watching the news and then writing tip 100. Also have them tell what they infer when Gloria is onstage alone, when the accident happens, and when Officer Buckle changes his mind. Take another look at the first page of the story and read the text; then ask children to infer how the officer comes up with his tips. As you bring this activity to a close, remind children that making inferences is an important reading strategy.

The Scoop on Safety

With *Officer Buckle and Gloria* as inspiration, motivating children to be on the lookout for safety tips is likely to be easy. In advance, gather newsletters, newspaper clippings, magazines, and other types of informational texts that feature brief safety tips. Introduce this activity by showing children the safety tips you found and explaining where you found them. Then ask each child to take home a copy of the note on page 69. For students who may have limited access to texts at home, place your safety tip references in a center along with a supply of magazines from which children can clip pictures of dogs. When the safety tips and dog pictures begin to arrive, help children post them on a magnetic surface at their eye level (such as the sides of a filing cabinet). If desired, provide one or two small star cutouts for each child to personalize, attach adhesive magnet strips to, and use to display his tip and canine cutout. Encourage students to read the tips during transition times. Then, when you have a few minutes to spare, guide children in discussing the tips they've read.

Safety Tip

Don't stand until the bus stops completely.

Trish

Tie Your Shoes

Keep your shoes tied so the laces don't cause you to fall.

Mel

Safety Officers at Work

Want your students to have a fine time researching and writing some safety tips? Explain that each student has just been appointed to be a new safety officer for a nearby school and that she has a canine sidekick, just as Officer Buckle does. Ask each child to find a helpful safety tip. (If your children participated in "The Scoop on Safety" they may use tips from the display as their references.) On writing paper, have the student write the tip and why it's a good idea to follow it (using her references as necessary).

For each child, provide a folded construction paper square bearing a half-star outline. Have her cut it out; then have her keep the paper folded as she trims, starting at the fold and going around the inside of the star shape as shown. A small star cutout and a larger star-shaped frame will result. Have her glue the frame to a contrasting color of construction paper and trim around the star, leaving a border of the contrasting color. Ask each child to personalize the smaller star and illustrate her canine companion, dramatizing the importance of the tip within the frame. Then have her attach the stars to her writing. When the projects are complete, encourage students to share their tips with their classmates, telling about the antics of their canine companions, the references they used to find the safety tip, and any personal experiences they have had with these tips.

#10
Don't run with SCISSORS in your hand.

#12
Don't play with MATCHES.

#15
Don't play with SPRAY CANS.

#18
Don't leave TENNIS BALLS on the STAIRS.

#21
Don't put ANYTHING in your EAR.

Write All About It

Recruit your students to be reporters for *The Napville News,* the newspaper of Officer Buckle's hometown, and they will eagerly apply their writing skills to the task. Begin by rereading *Officer Buckle and Gloria.* Then discuss with students what newspaper reporters do. Explain that reporters get assignments, interview sources, take notes, explain things in writing so that readers of the newspaper get all the important facts, and revise and edit their writing before it is published.

Distribute copies of page 70 and have each child choose an assignment to complete for the newspaper. Then encourage each child to write the first draft of his report. On another day, provide necessary support as each child revises and edits his work. If computers are available, suggest that some children may want to type the final drafts of their reports rather than write them by hand. When the reports are complete, ask volunteers for permission to publish their work and place it on a bulletin board or in a newsletter for their classmates.

Glories of Pet Ownership

Just as Gloria adds a new dimension to Officer Buckle's speeches, there are pets in your students' lives that add a world of warmth and fun. Begin this activity by asking students to describe how things are different after Gloria arrives and what it is about her that changes things. Then ask children to talk about their own pets (or ones they know of or would like to have) and explain why it's nice having them around. Encourage each child to write about a pet, including at least three things that he especially appreciates about it. Have each child glue his paper to a 9" x 12" sheet of construction paper and then fold it vertically in half to make a card. To the front of the card, have the child glue a 5" x 8" piece of contrasting construction paper. To complete the project, have him glue on a picture of the pet (or a drawing of the pet) and scraps of paper bearing the pet's name and his own. If desired, have students use stamps and stamp pads to embellish the outsides and insides of their cards. Encourage volunteers to display their projects for their classmates to enjoy.

Rex came to live with us in December. He was a silly pup at first. He's even crazier now. He's fun to play catch with. But he's the most fun when he bites our other dog's tail. Sometimes she barks at him. My favorite thing is when he sleeps in the bed with me. He keeps me warm.

Star Attraction

Gloria is the star of the safety show. But in this center your children can be star performers with making words. In advance, program each of six yellow star cutouts with a different letter to spell the word *safety*. Also program stars of three other colors to spell *officer, students,* and *accident.* Laminate and cut out the stars before attaching a strip of magnetic tape to the back of each. Place each color star in a different resealable plastic bag labeled with the word that the letters make; then put the bags, pencils, paper, and a cookie sheet in a center along with a copy of *Officer Buckle and Gloria.*

To use the center, have a child choose a bag, remove the programmed stars, and place them on the cookie sheet so that they spell a word from the story (referring to the label on the bag). Have him use some or all of the programmed stars to spell another word. Then have him note the word on a sheet of paper before moving the stars around to create another word and noting it. The child continues in this manner until he has made as many words from the letters as possible. Proofread (or have a classmate proofread) his work. Provide assistance with any misspellings. Encourage children to use more than one bag of stars each time they visit this center.

Dear Parents,

In school we are reading a book called *Officer Buckle and Gloria.* Ask your child to tell you the story. Officer Buckle gives speeches containing safety tips. Please assist your child in looking through magazines, newspapers, and other printed materials to find a safety tip. If your child finds a picture of a dog that he or she likes, please have him or her bring that picture to school. We will display the safety tips and dog pictures in our classroom for children to read and enjoy.

Please try to return a safety tip to school by _____.

Thanks for your help!

©The Education Center, Inc. • *Reading & Writing With Picture Books* • TEC1790

Dear Parents,

In school we are reading a book called *Officer Buckle and Gloria.* Ask your child to tell you the story. Officer Buckle gives speeches containing safety tips. Please assist your child in looking through magazines, newspapers, and other printed materials to find a safety tip. If your child finds a picture of a dog that he or she likes, please have him or her bring that picture to school. We will display the safety tips and dog pictures in our classroom for children to read and enjoy.

Please try to return a safety tip to school by _____.

Thanks for your help!

©The Education Center, Inc. • *Reading & Writing With Picture Books* • TEC1790

Assignments
Use with "Write All About It" on page 67.

Reporter:_____

Assignment 1 for *The Napville News*

Write about

Napville Police Department's New Canine Officer

Include the following:

- [ ] dog's name
- [ ] what she looks like
- [ ] what work she will do
- [ ] who she will work with

Reporter:_____

Assignment 2 for *The Napville News*

Write about

The Officer Buckle and Gloria Show

Include the following:

- [ ] where Officer Buckle speaks
- [ ] what Officer Buckle does
- [ ] what Gloria does
- [ ] how people respond

Reporter:_____

Assignment 3 for *The Napville News*

Write about

The Pudding Catastrophe

Include the following:

- [ ] the cause of the problem
- [ ] what happens to the children
- [ ] what happens to the principal
- [ ] what the children write about it

Reporter:_____

Assignment 4 for *The Napville News*

Write about

Officer Buckle's Return

Include the following:

- [ ] why Officer Buckle quits
- [ ] what makes him change his mind
- [ ] how people can contact him for a speech

Stellaluna

Written and illustrated by Janell Cannon

When the young bat Stellaluna becomes separated from her mother, she lands in an unlikely place—a bird's nest. Although the birds accept her into their family and enjoy the traits they have in common with her, they begin to notice that she has a few differences. She doesn't eat what they eat, rest as they rest, or fly when they fly. Stellaluna is downright different from her feathered friends. An unexpected turn of events soon proves that despite their differences, it's natural for them to remain friends.

Vocabulary

Swooping In on Vocabulary

Swoop into *Stellaluna* by focusing first on its rich vocabulary. To prepare, make ten copies of the bat cards on page 75. Cut out each card and program it with one of the words listed below. Then place the cards in a gift bag. When it's time to introduce the story, display the cover of *Stellaluna* and have children discuss what they think the book is about. Have each child take a card from the bag and then work with a partner to read the words, discuss their meanings, and contemplate how the words may be used in the story. Provide assistance as necessary. Lead into your first reading of *Stellaluna* by having partners read their words to their classmates, explain their meanings and how they determined them, and tell how they think the words relate to the story. Ask each child to listen for how his word is used in the story; then read the story. Afterward, revisit the vocabulary and discuss how the words are used and whether children need to revise any of their definitions.

What's the Meaning of This?

sultry	clutched	dodging	tangle	daybreak	downy
disappearing	curious	clambered	obey	gracefully	embarrassing
exercising	anxious	ached	peculiar	upside down	right side up
confused	murmured	escaped	survived	delicious	swooped
different	mystery	babble	dummy	alike	mango

A Quest for Questions

Use this activity to show your children how questions fuel our curiosity and deepen our understanding of what we've read. Reread *Stellaluna* and model for your students questions that come to mind as you focus on what the text is conveying. For example, the first sentence of the story might prompt you to wonder where the forests are that fruit bats live in, since the author mentions that they are far, far away. Write your question on a sticky note and attach it to the page near the text that brought the question to mind. Continue reading, thinking aloud, and adding sticky notes with questions for a few more pages, showing your students where questions naturally come to mind as you read. Gradually have the children do more of the thinking aloud and questioning as you continue through the book, adding sticky notes programmed with their questions.

After the book is read, your youngsters will see that they have many questions. Ask volunteers to find the answers with the assistance of the media specialist, older students, or parents. (See "Factually Speaking" for a related writing activity.) Revisit the book when most or all of the questions have been answered, and have the children explain what they have learned. It's amazing how much the questioning strategy improves comprehension of the story!

Why do bats han[g] upside down?

Were do fruit bats live?

Do owls eat bats?

What d[o] bats like to eat?

Factually Speaking

Help your children build their bat-related knowledge base by starting with what they have learned about bats in *Stellaluna* and building on that knowledge using related informational books. Before launching into this activity, ask your media specialist to help you gather several easy information books and children's articles about bats. Then talk with your students about aspects of *Stellaluna* that are fact and those that are fiction. Paraphrase the "bat notes" (at the end of the book) for children. Then encourage small groups to use the information books on hand to learn new facts about bats or to answer their own questions (such as the ones formulated in "A Quest for Questions"). Provide each child with a copy of one bat card (page 75) and writing paper. Have her write about something her group has learned about bats from the informational texts. Then have her color and cut out the bat pattern, fold its wings, and glue its body to her written work. Give children an opportunity to share what they have learned and relate it to *Stellaluna*.

Latoya

Some bats eat fruit and flowers. Their noses lead them to food. Some bats have pointed noses and very long tongues.

As Different As Night and Day

On nearly every page of *Stellaluna,* the author helps readers understand some of the contrasts between the habits of fruit bats and birds. Ahead of time, cut identical circles from white bulletin board paper. Add details to make one circle look like the moon and one to like like a nest. Display the circles on a bulletin board, shade the area of overlap with a highlighter, and label as shown.

After reading *Stellaluna* aloud, guide a discussion about the differences and similarities between Stellaluna and her bird friends. As children dictate, write habits or characteristics that are specific to fruit bats in the bat area and ones that are specific to birds in the bird area. Then discuss how they are alike and note their similarities in the overlapping area. Extend the learning by having students look at other books on birds and bats. As children learn new information about these creatures, have them add bat and bird facts near the display after decorating the facts with the bird and bat patterns from page 76.

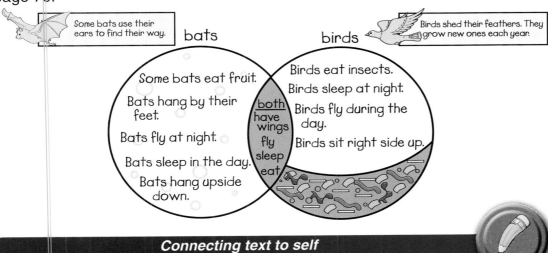

Some bats use their ears to find their way.

bats

birds

Birds shed their feathers. They grow new ones each year.

Some bats eat fruit.

Bats hang by their feet.

Bats fly at night.

Bats sleep in the day.

Bats hang upside down.

both have wings fly sleep eat

Birds eat insects.

Birds sleep at night.

Birds fly during the day.

Birds sit right side up.

Being Who You Are

Some things just come naturally to Stellaluna—others clearly don't. Skimming back through the book, have your youngsters recall at least three things that are easy for Stellaluna to do. Then ask each child to think about three things that he can do easily and successfully. Give each child a capital *I* cutout to glue near the top of a sheet of writing paper. Have him start with the word *I*, introducing himself and telling at least three things that he is good at. On the *I* cutout, have him glue a picture of himself and/or magazine pictures or drawings that relate to what he has written. When the writings are complete, have volunteers share their work with the class.

am Derrick. There are many things I'm good at. I am a good talker. I talk to kids. I talk to moms. I like to talk to Grandpa about playing ball. He says I'm a good shooter. I'm good at dribbling too.

Different and Alike

To help children personally connect with *Stellaluna*'s universal message, give these pennant-shaped writing projects a try. For each student, cut a 1½" x 30" poster board strip to represent a flagpole. Also cut large sheets of writing paper into pennant shapes, preparing two pennants per child.

Reread the last page of the story, in which the friends wonder aloud how they can be so different and so much alike at the same time. Then guide the conversation to help children think of friends (or relatives) with whom they have something special in common, even though they have very real differences. Provide each child with three sentence strips: one for the title "[Friend's name] and Me," one for writing how he and his friend are different, and one for writing how they are alike. After the strips are programmed, assist each child in taping his three strips to a flagpole as shown. Then provide the pennant-shaped paper and have each child elaborate on how he and his friend are alike and different. When the writing is complete, assist each child in taping his pennants to his flagpole. Pin the projects to a board so that the pennants seem to ripple in the wind.

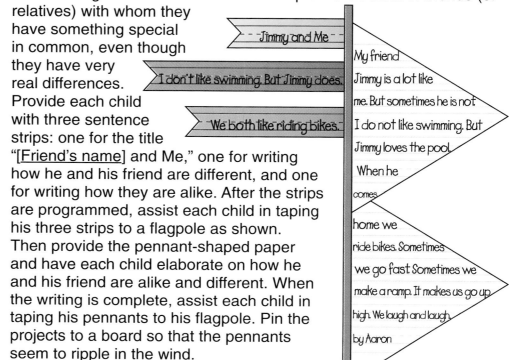

Jimmy and Me

I don't like swimming. But Jimmy does.

We both like riding bikes.

My friend Jimmy is a lot like me. But sometimes he is not. I do not like swimming. But Jimmy loves the pool. When he comes home we ride bikes. Sometimes we go fast. Sometimes we make a ramp. It makes us go up high. We laugh and laugh.
by Aaron

Is That Real?

Stellaluna contains an interesting combination of realistic and make-believe occurrences. At this center, have each child take another look at the book and determine which parts are realistic and which are not. Copy page 77 onto construction paper. Color-code the fronts of the category cards and the backs of the event cards for self-checking; then laminate them. Cut the cards apart and place them in a center along with the book. Model the center's use, reminding children to first take another look at the book and then read and sort the events from the story into two categories: real and make-believe. Show children how to check their answers using the color coding.

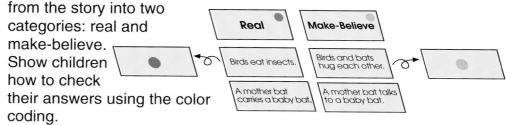

Real   **Make-Believe**

Birds eat insects.

Birds and bats hug each other.

A mother bat carries a baby bat.

A mother bat talks to a baby bat.

Bat Cards

Use with "Swooping In on Vocabulary" on page 71 and "Factually Speaking" on page 72.

©The Education Center, Inc.

©The Education Center, Inc.

©The Education Center, Inc.

Bat and Bird Patterns

Use with "As Different As Night and Day" on page 73.

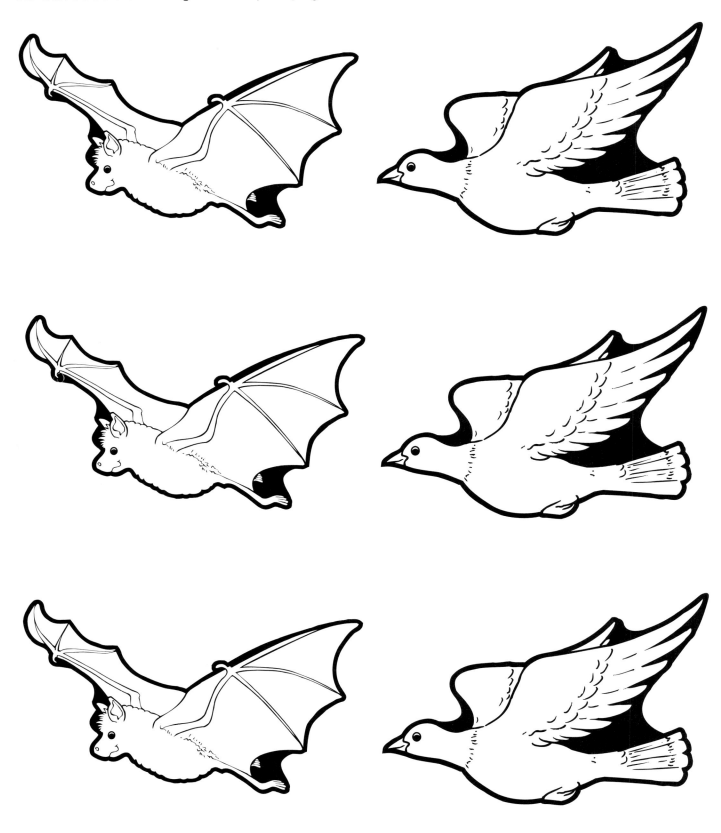

Real	Make-Believe
A mother bat carries a baby bat.	A mother bat talks to a baby bat.
Bats hang upside down.	A baby bat says, "Mother, where are you?"
Birds eat insects.	Baby birds hang upside down from their nest.
Baby birds jump from their nest to learn to fly.	A mother bird says, "You're going to fall and break your necks!"
Bats fly at night.	A bat saves birds from crashing at night.
Fruit bats eat mangoes.	Birds and bats hug each other.
Bats find their way in the dark.	A baby bat is fed by a mother bird.

Reading Skills Chart

Reading Skills	Rosie's Walk pp. 5–10	The Carrot Seed pp. 11–16	Whistle for Willie pp. 17–22	Noisy Nora pp. 23–28	Where the Wild Things Are pp. 29–34	Seven Blind Mice pp. 35–40	The Cat in the Hat pp. 41–46	Harry the Dirty Dog pp. 47–52	Zomo the Rabbit: A Trickster Tale From West Africa pp. 53–58	Miss Nelson Is Missing! pp. 59–64	Officer Buckle and Gloria pp. 65–70	Stellaluna pp. 71–77
activating prior knowledge										●		
asking questions												●
capitalization and punctuation			●									
cause and effect	●								●			
choral reading				●								
classifying words						●						
comparing and contrasting										●		●
connecting text to self								●				
contrasting characters	●											
describing a character							●					
dramatization		●			●							
extending the text						●						
fact and opinion									●			
identifying with characters									●			
letter-sound correspondence			●									
listening for a purpose							●				●	
making inferences											●	
making words											●	
opposites											●	
prediction	●		●									
reading for details						●						
reading for meaning			●									
reading informational texts											●	
reality and fantasy					●							●
recalling	●			●								
retelling						●						
rhyming words							●					
sequencing					●		●	●	●	●		
story innovation		●										
syllables		●										
synonyms				●								
vocabulary				●				●				●
word recognition					●							

Writing Skills Chart

Writing Skills Chart	Rosie's Walk pp. 5–10	The Carrot Seed pp. 11–16	Whistle for Willie pp. 17–22	Noisy Nora pp. 23–28	Where the Wild Things Are pp. 29–34	Seven Blind Mice pp. 35–40	The Cat in the Hat pp. 41–46	Harry the Dirty Dog pp. 47–52	Zomo the Rabbit: A Trickster Tale From West Africa pp. 53–58	Miss Nelson Is Missing! pp. 59–64	Officer Buckle and Gloria pp. 65–70	Stellaluna pp. 71–77
connecting text to self			●	●	●		●	●	●			●
descriptive words	●											
developing a central idea			●								●	
expository writing											●	
extending the text								●		●		
gaining perspective						●						
letter writing				●						●		
making connections between texts												●
making inferences										●		
points of view						●						
prepositional phrases	●											
process writing											●	
quotation marks		●										
recalling								●				
sequencing		●										
story innovation									●			
visualizing						●						
word families		●		●								
writing about imaginary things					●							
writing descriptive sentences		●					●					
writing dialogue	●											
writing in complete sentences			●					●	●			

Answer Keys

Page 39
first, red
second, green
third, yellow
fourth, purple
fifth, orange
sixth, blue
seventh, white

Page 42
cat
hat
fat
mat
flat
that
sat
fish
dish
wish
box
fox
ox
play
say
hay
lay
day
thing
bring
sing
wing
king

Page 63

1.  Miss Swamp
2. Miss Nelson
3. Miss Nelson
4. Miss Swamp
5. Miss Swamp
6. Miss Nelson
7. Miss Nelson
8. Miss Swamp

Bonus Box: Answers will vary.